Max Weber

S. M. MILLER

Syracuse University

THOMAS Y. CROWELL COMPANY

New York, Established 1834

Editor's Foreword

Undergraduates often find a great challenge in reading a seminal thinker's major contributions to social science in their original form. But students are usually offered either volume-length works containing stimulating passages embedded in outworn discussions, or brief excerpts included with those of other authors in general collections of readings. The longer works tend to be repetitious and wordy, and some now appear misguided. At the same time, excerpts in general collections do not give enough of a contributor's work to make him come alive.

In planning the present series, John T. Hawes, Director of the College Department of the Thomas Y. Crowell Company, and I sought manuscripts free from either of the above weaknesses. The editors were asked to dig out the main lines of a contributor's method and thought from the verbiage and the dated materials obscuring them, and to make available, in one slim volume, a critical essay together with the most significant and interesting passages in a contributor's writings. The volumes in the series, considered as a whole, thus give the student an understanding of the diverse ways of thought that have gone into the making of the social science discipline as we now know it.

The series has been edited and written so that each little book can be read for its own merits and without need of additional props. Each contains the seminal ideas of an author which still remain alive today but does not gloss over his weaknesses. Each book provides a critical vignette of the social scientist as he is now seen. Each book, too, should be interesting to college sophomores and especially to undergraduate majors in the various social sciences.

What all volumes in the series have in common is an educative conception. They are all efforts to interest undergraduates in some of the great "originals" of social science and thus to stimulate further exploration of important ideas and methods. The editor-critic who has done each volume has been free to follow his own professional judgment in analyzing his major contributor and in selecting significant excerpts from his works. Each volume thus has an individuality deriving from its editor-critic as well as from its subject.

The books in this series are intended to enrich introductory courses in the various social sciences. For more advanced courses, they will permit the student to become acquainted with the meatiest contributions of many selected social scientists rather than the few whose works he might read more extensively. Advanced students will find these books invaluable for the purposes of review.

ALFRED MC CLUNG LEE

Preface

This book aims to provide a compact introduction to the widely ranging work of one of the most profound thinkers of the twentieth century. Intended primarily for introductory sociology, social science, and political science courses and for theory courses in sociology and political science, it will perhaps have applications also to courses in public administration, the sociology of organization, social stratification, political sociology, and the sociology of religion. Its major use may well be as a way of inducing students who have heard of Weber to actually read him. This convenient compilation of presently available translations will best justify itself by encouraging the student to read Weber more fully in the twelve volumes of his writings that have been published in English.

The first two chapters display Weber's theoretical and methodological approaches. The selections in Chapter 1 discuss the concepts that are fundamental to Weber's analysis, centering on his interpretation of "social relationship." The following chapter deals with his use of the tool of the ideal-type. These approaches are then employed in Chapter 3, which presents selections from Weber's most famous work, *The Protestant Ethic and the Spirit of Capitalism*. This chapter is followed by selections from his comparative religion studies, which develop the theme of *The Protestant Ethic*. Much of Weber's current influence rests in his analysis of social stratification and the political order; consequently, the readings in Chapter 5 are from the well-known discussion of class, status, and party; they are followed in Chapter 6 by the analysis of the sources and types of political legitimacy, tradition, charisma, and bureaucracy. The final chapter deals with some of Weber's penetrating comments on the German political scene which havce significance for today.

The complexity of Weber's writing makes it difficult to provide selections both cohesive and representative of his broad interests. Since Weber proliferated examples and elaborations, it is frequently difficult to capture the essence of his argument. At a number of places (especially in "The Protestant Ethic" and "The Political Scene"), the editor has presumed to cut and splice together Weber's writing to organize a more manageable and compact presentation. Where this has been done, page notes follow the paragraphs to indicate the relevant pages in the source.

An extremely useful guide to Weber has been recently published; in his *Max Weber: An Intellectual Portrait*, Reinhard Bendix has skillfully and creatively woven together many of the complex strands of Weber's analysis. The "Bibliographical Note" in that book contains a listing of Weber's work in English translation. Gerth and Mills, Parsons, and Rheinstein in their editorial introductions to various volumes of Weber in translation have provided useful interpretations. Parsons' chapters on Weber in his *The Structure of Social Action* are very valuable. H. Stuart Hughes' *Consciousness and Society*, which provides an excellent introduction to European thought at the turn of the century, is particularly interesting on Weber.

The following have helpfully commented on the Introduction: Abraham Ascher, Seymour S. Bellin, Norman Birnbaum, Lewis Coser, Samuel Hurwitz, Alfred McClung Lee, Elizabeth Thompson, and Kurt H. Wolff. I have not always been able to take advantage of their suggestions and they, of course, bear no responsibility for the Introduction and the choice of selections.

S.M.M.

Syracuse, N.Y.
January, 1963

Contents

Introduction

Max Weber has become one of the monumental figures of social science. His sociological and political concepts are part of the working vocabulary of social scientists. The work of this man of encyclopedic knowledge has illumined several fields of sociology and political science and is of special importance in the study of economic history and in the investigation of the links between religion and society.

WEBER'S LIFE

Weber was born in 1864 and died in 1920. His life thus spanned the emergence of the German nation and its defeat in World War I. He had a broadly ranging mind and a historical bent, but his outlook was heavily influenced by the immediate events of German life.

Like many other scholars of Germany, he was born in a family of affluence, with considerable political and social connections.* His family was of the upper middle class, and his father was a figure in German politics, supporting the National-Liberals, the party of the business groups. Leading intellectual and political personages frequented their home. This atmosphere led to the kind of intellectual concern and drive that produced Max Weber and his brother, Alfred, also an outstanding sociologist.

Weber, as Gerth and Mills have pointed out, was a product of the gymnasium, the preuniversity school, where outstanding teachers fur-

* The following account is indebted to the stimulating notes of Hans Gerth and C. Wright Mills in *From Max Weber* (New York: Oxford University Press, 1946) and of Reinhard Bendix in his *Max Weber: An Intellectual Portrait* (Garden City: Doubleday & Company, Inc., 1960).

thered curiosity, depth, and breadth among students of talent. At an early age, Weber was reading complex philosophical works with critical acumen.

His university career was varied. The German university system permits a student to move from one university to another with comparative ease. Weber entered the University of Heidelberg in 1882 as a student of law. At nineteen, he moved to Strasbourg where he served his one-year army term and spent much time with the family of his uncle, who was a minister. Subsequently he resumed his studies, attending the universities of Berlin and Göttingen, and also had several brief periods of further military service. He took his first law examination in 1886 and was then attached to the Berlin law courts.

He continued his studies at the University of Berlin and in 1889 wrote a Ph.D. thesis entitled "A Contribution to the History of Medieval Business Organization," an analysis of the impact of legal regulations on economic activities. In 1891, he formally qualified ("habilitation") for the rank of dozent (instructor) in Roman, German, and commercial law by completing "Roman Agrarian History and Its Significance for Public and Private Law," an interpretation of Roman society. Theodor Mommsen, the renowned Roman historian, commented at the academic defense of Weber's work that this student was the man to succeed him in his chair.

Weber packed the next few years with work. He lectured widely and served several government offices as consultant. For a professional organization (Verein für Sozialpolitik), he studied rural labor in East Prussia and in 1892 published a large volume on this subject. His analysis of the stock exchange was published the following year. As Bendix has pointed out, both studies had common themes: (1) the two-sided cutting edge of commercialization which created new, potentially liberating cultural values but destroyed old, stabilizing ones; (2) the importance of social and personal motives and ethics—in short, of ideas—in economic conduct.

In 1893, he married his cousin, Marianne Schnitger, and the following year, at only thirty, he became a full professor of economics at Freiburg University. In 1896, he moved to the University of Heidelberg, replacing the famous economic historian Knies. His friends and colleagues were men of great prominence in German intellectual life.

One year later, at the age of thirty-three, he collapsed and could not fulfill his university duties. For the next four years, he was in a state of depression, unable to work, even to read. For a short period, he stayed in a mental institution. He traveled considerably, especially in Italy, and gradually resumed his studying. Intermittently throughout the rest of his life, however, he had periods of biting depression.

In 1902, he returned to Heidelberg but could not maintain the load of full teaching responsibilities. He insisted on resigning his chair and assuming the role of lecturer. Weber continued to travel and suffered repeated anxieties and strains. In 1903, he was well enough to join Werner Sombart and Edgar Jaffé in editing what became the leading social-science journal in Germany, Archiv für Sozialwissenschaft und Sozialpolitik (Archives for Social Science and Social Welfare). He thus reentered the mainspring of German scholarship and began his great creative period, publishing in 1904 the first part of The Protestant Ethic and the Spirit of Capitalism, as well as essays on the Junkers and on objectivity in the social sciences. Unlike many other outstanding scholars, who were young when they began their most significant work, Weber was thirty-eight when his great intellectual productivity commenced. He had suffered much and had prevailed.

Weber continued to work at Heidelberg, though refusing a chair. In 1907, an inheritance freed him from his dependence on the financial assistance of the university. He then lived the life of a private scholar, reading and writing widely, participating in the political as well as the intellectual life of Germany. He served briefly in World War I as an administrator of an army hospital in Heidelberg; in 1918, he was a consultant to the German Armistice Commission at the Versailles negotiations. In the summer of 1918, he taught at the University of Vienna—his first full course of lectures in more than fifteen years. The following year he accepted a chair at the University of Munich; his lectures were provocative and warmly received. He contributed to the drafting of the Weimer Constitution and hoped, unsuccessfully, to have a high political post in the new republic. In 1920, he died during the influenza epidemic. Between 1902 and his death, he had written an enormous amount on a wide range of topics; much of his writing appeared posthumously and in incomplete form.

THE GERMAN BACKGROUND

Weber was of the great breed of exceedingly erudite ninteteenth century German scholars who maintained a persistent theme throughout their prolific writings in a wide range of fields. Frequently, they were passionately committed men deeply concerned with the course of German politics and national life. Weber, a young man when Marx died, was of a generation that grew up in a Germany recently united and swiftly industrializing—despite feudalistic restraints. The new Germany was a political cauldron with strong left, center, and right movements surrounding a power-oriented monarchy. This setting deeply affected Weber's work.

Three great developments occurred in Germany in Weber's lifetime. Germany became a national state rather than a series of principalities, duchies, and kingdoms; industrialization moved ahead rapidly in this new nation; imperialism and Continental (European) supremacy— the development of overseas colonies, the increasing economic reliance of several nations on Germany, the use of military force, the importance of national pacts—became state policy.

These developments were fused in a society that had a strong, governmental bureaucracy, an autocratic and incompetent Kaiser in Wilhelm II, and a complex interplay of political and economic interests. Because of their central role in Prussia, the aristocratic Junkers, whose economic base was agriculture, were the dominant influence in the German Empire. As the Social Democratic (working-class) party increasingly won support and the Center (Catholic) party played an oppositionist role, the Junkers (Conservative Party) were forced into a working arrangement with the leading industrial groups who were in the Liberal Party. This industrial elite, in turn, went through a process of "refeudalization" in which they sought honorific titles, entailed estates, and the like as markers of acceptance into traditional high society. The Junkers, however, developed more "capitalist" modes of exploiting their extensive lands, including the importing of cheap labor of Polish extraction. When joining with the Liberals to support tariffs, however, they used the cloak of traditionalism to win support for measures aimed at narrow economic gain.*

---

* In his analysis of East Prussia rural labor, Weber strongly objected to importing Polish agricultural workers for he felt that the need for a strong, ethnically integrated nation should override economic interests.

Germany, beset by many competing forces, was a society of tension held together by the Junker-capitalist alliance and the idea of the national state. Contradictory tendencies abounded. Despite the state socialism of Bismarck aimed at welding the worker to the state rather than to unions and militant political forms, the government was capable of great disregard for workers' rights and maintained discriminatory voting arrangements. Many German academicians, proud of their deep sense of the complexity of history, were ardent patriots supporting the German "mission" to spread its culture.

The course of industrialization was more rapid in Germany than it had been in England, France, and even the United States. In "coming last" as Thorstein Veblen put it, Germany had the advantage of taking over technology at its highest level of development (rather than having some factories and mines with antiquated equipment as was then beginning to happen in Britain). "Incrustations," built-up social customs limiting the use of machines, were not adopted along with the technology. Consequently, the new nation could move along rapidly, at least until incrustations became more important.

While Germany had the advantage of using high technology, it had a besetting political problem. In England, the Glorious Revolution and later the Anti-Corn Law movement had been part of the effort of the rising merchants and industrialists to win political support to overcome the restrictions placed upon their activities by the ruling elite of agriculture. In France, the revolutions of 1789 and 1830 marked the similar effort of the urban, industrial, and commercial elites to win political power commensurate with their economic power. In both nations, the battle had been largely won fairly early in the industrialization process. In the United States, the Civil War marked the political supremacy of the manufacturing North over the plantation South.

In the newly established Germany, no such dramatic events occurred during its compressed economic development: The Junkers retained considerable political power despite the rise of the capitalists, and the marriage of this military-agricultural group to the advanced technology encouraged the imperialistic activities of Germany and promoted a bellicose spirit. The superimposition of capitalism upon Prussia's strained agricultural structure meant that Germany did not experience the social and agricultural revolutions (the shifts in political power between classes; the breakup of large estates) usually associated with the development of capitalism.

German sociologists and philosophers were deeply concerned with the decline and breakdown of the small, primary, face-to-face community, and its replacement with the large, impersonal, secondary city. Tönnies analyzed the differences between "Community" and "Society" (Gemeinschaft and Gesellschaft); later, Spengler explored the dangers of the megalopolis which signified for him "the decline of the West." Intellectuals in other nations had somewhat similar concerns, but the Germans were particularly drawn to this issue because the old community had not been largely destroyed in the early days of capitalism. The old and new stood side by side in Germany, although the old was being destroyed at a rapid rate in this short period of burgeoning industrialism.

This ambivalence about the traditional and the new was pronounced in Weber himself. He saw the development of capitalism on a wide screen, and much of his work focused on a major theme which embraced capitalism as only one manifestation of the tendency toward the increasing rationalization of life. His studies of religion, bureaucracy, law, and music all illustrated the decline of traditional and magical practices and the substitution of systematic, reasoned, purposive, and secular modes of behavior. Weber saw the efficiency side of rationalization, the emphasis on choosing the most effective means of gaining a given end. But he was also concerned with the other side of the coin—the destruction of traditional values, increasing alienation from a rationalized society, the need for integrating symbols and leaders. The "disenchantment" of the world resulted from giving up the old and traditional for the rational and was the price paid for progress, but Weber was not always sure that the return was worth the cost.

Weber was, in a sense, the Adam Smith of Germany; a century and more after Smith, he too was concerned with the development of industrialization in his country. Smith, in his volume on The Wealth of Nations (1776), ushered in a new economics concerned with the dynamics of capitalism and critical of the retarding impact in Britain of governmentally supported mercantilist practices of restriction. In his early work Weber discussed the negative role of legal provisions regulating estates held in trust, the aristocratic pretensions of the rising capitalist class, and the Junkers' manipulation of political power to permit them to employ foreign farm workers. These steps, according to Weber, encouraged business ethics incompatible with the needs of capitalism; political control was used to support a ruling class that no longer had a strong economic base and whose economic interests were in conflict with national interests. Like Smith, the general thrust of Weber's work was to outline the political, economic, and psychological requirements of a new capitalist state.

WEBER AND MARX

Touching the political ferment in Germany at various points was the intellectual tug-of-war between idealists and materialists, between those who—to put the argument in its barest form—emphasized the independent role of ideas in shaping history and those who stressed the primacy of the material conditions of life in shaping ideas and history.

Much of what Weber wrote was in relationship to Marxism; as Albert Salomon put it, he engaged in a lifelong dialogue with the ghost of Marx. The Protestant Ethic, for example, was aimed at emphasizing ideological or motivational factors that were understressed by the Marxists. The analysis of class was, again, an attempt to introduce analytic variables that were conventionally neglected in the economic emphasis of the Marxists. The Weberian stress on bureaucracy and its development in industrial society was partly an effort to show that alienation, the other side of rationalization, was not exclusively a product of capitalism but could be brought about in many different kinds of societies, including socialist ones.

To Marx's emphasis on the mode of production as determining relations in society, Weber wished to add the character of political power and organization as important determinants. In his economic history, Weber emphasized the effect of military factors in order to show that narrow economic forces were not all-important. For Weber, the charismatic leader as well as the economic generator were the engines of history.

It was not that Weber felt that economic forces were insignificant. No one (at least no German scholar) concerned with economic history is likely to disregard economic pressures. Rather, Weber felt that the historical materialism of his day was one-sided, neglecting the interplay of economic forces with political, military, social, and psychological pressures. The materialist approach might be a first approximation, but only that. If one were concerned with concrete historical events, as Weber was, it was necessary to look at a broader spectrum of determinants of action.

At times, it appears that Weber felt that the noneconomic forces were the only compelling ones, but those paragraphs seem to be rhetorical, written to dramatize a point. In defending his position in The Protestant Ethic, he declared that he realized the significance of economic forces and was not denigrating them by arguing that noneconomic events play a role in capitalist development. He asserted that he did not wish to substitute a one-sided ideational position for a one-sided economic one. Marx and Engels were similarly caught in extreme positions, and, as Engels wrote in a famous letter to Kugelmann, they overstated their materialist analysis in order to argue against prevailing tendencies. Weber, faced as he saw it with narrow Marxist analyses, also exaggerated his position and stressed heavily the role of noneconomic factors. Although he never wrote a full equivalent of a letter to Kugelmann, he clearly tried to avoid the underevaluation of economic forces. Indeed, he was at pains in The Protestant Ethic and elsewhere to point out that his mode of investigation was first to single out the specific class groupings in society that played a major role in developing new religions and then to explain the origins of the content of their views.

Nonetheless, Weber is frequently viewed as an anti-Marxian. This interpretation stresses the polemical (and political) aspects of his work. An alternative view sees Weber as attempting to include the Marxian categories in his mode of analysis but not to be satisfied with them alone. To see Weber mainly as an "anti" figure tends to stultify our enrichment of the legacy that he left. Seminal thinkers tend to be controversial, and a good deal of argument is expended in defending or opposing them. A. G. Hart, a leading American economist, has offered sage advice on this matter in his discussion of John Maynard Keynes, the challenging English economist. The important issue, Hart declared, is not whether an economist is pro-Keynesian or anti-Keynesian. The more appropriate category of classification is whether one is pre-Keynesian or post-Keynesian. In these terms of utilizing but not being bound by intellectual predecessors, Weber was a post-Marxian.

MODES OF ANALYSIS

Weber conceived and planned a comprehensive series of books to be written by many scholars and aimed at analyzing the interrelationships of society and economy. He wrote Wirtschaft und Gesellschaft (Economy and Society) to introduce the series. In this incomplete and posthumously published work, Weber outlined useful terms and concepts of analysis. He gave voluminous historical examples but did not present a systematic interweaving of the concepts. Weber's aim was not to invent a new vocabulary for novelty's sake. He wished to delineate carefully the varied dimensions of a number of issues (social relationships, bureaucracy, class, economic categories) and to provide ways of talking about them. He recognized that classifications mold and direct thought and analysis.

Terminological niceties and classificatory systems often are barren and dry as dust, coining new words for tired ideas. But they can also be productive if they provide useful packing boxes for the differentiating and ordering of ideas. Only when they are concretely employed can they be evaluated: Do they provide serviceable "handles" for grasping problems? Some of the following selections on authority and social class indicate terminological clarifications established by Weber which have had a great and generally positive impact on the work of his successors. A set of terminological distinctions which is productive appears to be characterized by (1) abstraction from empirical events (as with Weber's categories) and (2) refinement through application (as with some but not all of Weber's specifications).

Weber's attempt to distinguish the character of social relationships has been particularly influential. Contemporary thinking was muddled in its analysis of human society. Some writers utilized a "social will" in their analysis and made no attempt to relate this grand organic conception to the concrete ideas of individual members of society. Others spoke about the impersonal pressure of the material structure of society as determining relationships. Weber tried to avoid the difficulties of reification (treating abstractions as though they were material things) and the superorganic approach which ignored the concrete processes of society. He argued that the social relationship was the basic unit of society. His emphasis in the definition of this concept was that the actors take account of or are oriented to one another. Social action consequently is motivated— that is, the actors each have a subjective meaning associated with every act. An important task of the sociologist is, therefore, to discover these meanings. "Verstehen" was the term employed by Weber to describe the intricate process of interpretation involved.

The stress on the subjective meaning of the action for the individual was part of a concern for norms. For the logical question that followed from emphasis on the subjective was: How do meanings become patterned so that certain meanings can be expected in certain situations?

One tool that Weber employed to help in the clarification of this and other problems was the "ideal type." As he used it, the "ideal" did not refer to a desirable condition but to a pure one. For example, traditional, charismatic, and legal-rational forms of authority are seldom found to exist in an unalloyed state; various combinations of them are found in the concrete situations of the real world. But to understand the combinations, it is necessary, Weber argued, to know what each strand is like in itself.

The ideal type is thus an abstraction and can be useful as one. When it is employed as a description of empirical events, it is inadmissible. Used properly as a tool and not as a crutch—when it points to relevant things to study rather than to conclusions to be drawn —it may be valuable.

Weber's concern with Verstehen and ideal types was part of his solution to the perplexing philosophical and historical contentions in Germany during his lifetime. Was social life amenable to scientific analysis? How did values and intuition fit into the social sciences? Were conceptions of causality compatible with those of free will and irrationality? Was the social scientists' major role to collect facts or to develop generalizations? And if the latter, how embracing should the generalization be? Did Romanticism with such notions as "folk soul" have a contribution to make? As H. Stuart Hughes has pointed out in his stimulating and useful book Consciousness and Society (New York, Alfred A. Knopf, Inc., 1959), Weber's categories of analysis do not seem the most useful part of his work. Perhaps this is due to their emergence within and relevance for the distinctive German intellectual traditions of the nineteenth century.

RELIGION AND SOCIETY

The best known of Max Weber's writings are his studies in the sociology of religion. They began with his monograph on the Protestant ethic and its relationship to the development of capitalism. In later studies he attempted to support his thesis by examining the role of religion in the ancient societies of India, China, and Palestine.

In The Protestant Ethic, Weber attempted to show the influence of the Calvinist tradition on the development of the psychology or motivation appropriate for the nature of capitalism. He argued that an acquisitive spirit, a drive for money, an effort to accumulate profit, is not unique to this economic system. Rather, what characterizes it is a rational economic spirit, a freedom from restraints of traditionalism. In short, Weber argued that capitalism requires a particular kind of psychology in which people are not only willing to work hard, but also are willing to innovate, to save the funds they have acquired, and to reinvest them in business enterprise. Further, he argued that this kind of outlook was uniquely provided by Protestantism. He did not argue that it was Protestantism alone that produced capitalism, but rather that, given the "sufficient" economic preconditions for capitalism, the religion produced the "necessary" motivation so that the new economic form could emerge.

Weber was not alone in his concern with the emergence of a capitalist mentality, for Werner Sombart had also tackled this problem and had concluded that an outsider group, the Jews, provided the unique constellation of attitudes that permitted capitalism to appear. It is interesting to speculate why these German social scientists were concerned with this problem. Their society had only recently narrowed the tremendous contrasts between important groups in regard to a capitalistic mentality. The rising burgher interests of the city had manifested the rational capitalist outlook at the same time that the politically and socially powerful Junker class based upon the land had exhibited the traditional outlook of a precapitalist era. German society was rent between the old and new, the patterns of the economically declining but still socially and politically strong nobility and the needs of the emerging economically powerful groups. In this situation, the significance of the orientation of thought characteristic of capitalism was starkly etched for German sociologists.

From this perspective, Weber attempted to go beyond Marx.

While he agreed with Marx that certain economic conditions were necessary for the development of capitalism, he felt that Marx and his successors had ignored the necessity of a particular psychology which would permit the crystallization of new forms of economic activity. This crystallization was provided by Protestantism. Weber's analysis was no crude mechanical affair in which he argued that Protestantism directly gave birth to an economic spirit that was desirable for capitalism. Rather he argued that parallel to the development of certain economic forms in late medieval Europe was the rise of a new kind of outlook upon the world which was adopted by the rising middle classes. The concern with intense worldly activity as signs and harbingers of salvation emerged from the asceticism of Calvinism and Puritanism. Unlike Catholicism, those churches did not make economic activity unworthy. In his detailed studies of the evolution of Protestant sects, he sought to show how theological dogma became individual motivation.

Weber sought to support his contentions by analyzing the role of the religious factor in other societies. He argued that a number of societies had an economic base not dissimilar to that of precapitalist Europe, yet in these societies full capitalist development did not emerge. Why was this so? His answer was that the characteristic religions of these societies did not encourage the intense economic activity which Protestantism did. In India, for example, he showed how Hinduism supported a rigid caste system which operated against the possibility of the changing economic tide. And he made similar points in analyzing ancient Palestine and China.

Weber's thesis of Protestantism has resulted in a welter of criticism and discussion by historians and other social scientists. Two principal arguments against Weber are that his concept of capitalism is limited and that his theory does not explain the actual ecology of capitalism in Western Europe. Further, his notion of "precapitalist" economic conditions is not specified, and it is doubtful whether ancient India, Palestine, and China shared with Western Europe the same agricultural, political, social structural, and technological conditions for movement into a capitalist form. Another contention that has been offered is that Catholicism had changed so considerably in practice that by the beginning of the capitalist era it was not a barrier to the emergence of a new mode of economic conduct.

The importance of religious values in affecting the behavior of emerging capitalists has also been challenged. One form of this position is the assertion that Protestantism was a response to changing economic conditions rather than an independent influence on them. On Weber's side is the evidence Protestants were disproportionately involved in science and business activity in Germany and Britain and that rational capitalism was initially restricted to a few areas of the world.* To evaluate Weber's thesis is most difficult. The issue is probably not whether religious forces played a decisive role, but how much influence they exercised in which situations.

Even if Weber is wrong, his analysis is extremely useful. It shows the power of a comparative approach and demonstrates how historical and sociological analyses can be interwoven. Considerable research into the relations between religion and society has resulted. The theoretical point which animated Weber is of great importance: We cannot assume that from the given nature of an institution an appropriate psychology will automatically emerge. The "appropriate" psychology, which may not always appear, may have to be produced, at least in part, by other institutional complexes in society.

Anthropologists have tended to support the Weberian notion in arguing that "the cake of custom" in many new nations was so intact and strong that economic development could not take place until traditional values were dislodged. More recently some have contended, on the contrary, that the anthropological emphasis on the constraint and stability of traditionalism has been exaggerated and that the relative few in a society who have to develop a new economic outlook are able to do so in fairly rapid order.

The last words in this controversy have not been heard.

SOCIAL STRATIFICATION

Weber's conceptualization of social stratification plays an important role in present-day analysis. Weber started from a Marxian premise but put the Marxian approach into a larger framework, adding political and social dimensions to the discussion. Since he was not mainly concerned with the working class, the scope of his analysis included the middle classes, largely residual categories in Marxian analysis.

* Kurt Samuelsson has challenged the data for Germany. See his *Religion and Economic Action* (New York: Basic Books Publishing Company, 1961), pp. 137–49.

With Marx, he recognized the importance of the economic (or, in current terminology, the "class") basis of stratification in society, but he placed a different emphasis on the economic factor. Marx's concern was with ownership, the relation to the means of production, whereas Weber's stress was on the market as of crucial importance for the conduct of the individual's life. On the one hand, according to Marx, workers' property rights had been prevented from developing and workers consequently were exploited by the capitalist. Weber, on the other hand, emphasized the workers' inability to compete successfully in the market with the capitalist and with other economic agents. He stressed the nature of the "life chances" of individuals in particular economic situations. Weber's treatment of the economic aspect of social stratification is more refined in many ways than the Marxian.

Weber saw stratification as broader than the purely economic process. A status dimension was important. Perhaps, living in Germany impressed him with the role of honor and with the importance of the styles of life associated with particular classes and particular situations. He recognized that individuals could aspire to models of conduct and consumption which were inconsonant with their economic or social background. The nouveau riche pattern, for example, characterizes a group attempting to adopt a behavioral mode which they hope will win them high social position. Seymour S. Bellin has suggested that Marx largely ignored honor and prestige as a dimension of stratification because he saw such concerns as vestigial remains of a dying precapitalist thought; Weber, living in a later stage of industrialization, saw the institutionalized patterning of and striving for prestige in the more highly developed capitalist societies.

The political or power realm formed a third dimension of the stratification system, paralleling the class and status orders. The German experience may have influenced Weber to stress that political power was not an automatic concomitant of economic power. The political order was to some extent at least independent of the other two orders. Consequently, it was necessary to analyze concretely the sources and character of the political power of different groupings rather than inferring political behavior and power from knowledge of the other orders.

Weber's broadened extension of class has had an influential role in the analysis of stratification in recent years. The work in stratification in the United States and the prestige dimension of social class has been an important focus of study, but, as C. Wright Mills indicated in a very important review of W. Lloyd Warner's work, this is only one of its dimensions. In recent years, this inordinate stress on prestige has continued, but emphasis has shifted to the style of life (consumption style) aspect. In market-research studies, populations have been stratified on this variable; discussions of "high brow, middle brow, and low brow" essentially pertain to the style of life variable. Weber's concern with the political dimension of stratification has been given new attention in the last decade, sparked especially by the work of S. M. Lipset.

Weber sees economic stratification, not as isolated from the social and political dimension, but as intimately connected with them; social and political conditions can affect the nature of the economic response to a given situation. Here, as elsewhere, Weber was concerned with the interrelatedness of the varied institutional orders of society, although he did not systematically explore the interaction of these orders. Few of his successors have undertaken this task, although Mills' The Power Elite and Vidich and Bensman's Small Town in Mass Society are important exceptions since they are conscious attempts by Weberians to see the links of economic, political, and social variables. The collection of essays edited by Daniel Bell, The New Radical Right, is specifically concerned with depicting the role of status concerns in political behavior.

The interactions of these variables will be of great importance in newly industrializing societies where old forms of society and stratification mingle with new. Weber's approach to the study of stratification will probably continue to play a central role, as the linkages among the variables become of central concern.

POWER AND BUREAUCRACY

Perhaps Weber's most lasting contribution will be his stress on bureaucracy. Weber characteristically was concerned with the State, a legitimated (i.e., socially accepted) organ which monopolizes military power and pursues national objectives. He traced the different sources of authority of legitimated power: the traditional, the charismatic, and the legal-rational. The selections in this volume present some indication of how he used these terms.

In his analysis, he greatly stressed the charismatic leader, the man of compelling personality and mystik, who was able to compel the attention and support of great numbers. Social movements could be depicted in terms of the dramatic individual who epitomized the movement and was able to bring it to fruition. Perhaps Weber's concept of the charismatic leader was part of his attempt to show the importance of the hero in history, while recognizing that he is not the sole pressure in the historical picture. Whatever the intent, Weber's emphasis—not unlike that of Nietzsche—breaks in part with the Marxian stress on the impact of economic forces.

One way of viewing Weber's stress on the charismatic leader is that he saw this leader as emerging at nodal points in history when traditional or bureaucratic authority was decaying. The charismatic leader galvanized support and assumed power; in turn, his power and appeal became routinized so that his successors could assume control. In time, the effectiveness of the followers was weakened, and they were eventually supplanted by new charismatic leaders. This speculative interpretation implies a rather cyclical theory of history, but Weber generally eschewed the kind of grand theory which captured many other theorists of his time. In any case, his discussion of charisma and its institutionalization has added new dimensions to the study of authority.

Bureaucracy is generally derived from the legal-rational form of authority. The decline of traditionalism and the growth of rationality were associated with the movement toward a bureaucratic form of administration in all fields, not only in government. Although bureaucracy represented a considerable advance since it was designed for efficiency, it could produce alienation (from the means of administration, rather than from the means of production, as in Marx's analysis).

Weber at several points outlines the characteristics of bureaucracy. His approach is essentially formal, outlining the blueprint character of bureaucracy—the rule of rules rather than of men, the role of hierarchy, specialization, and experience, the development of the office as a career.

He did not analyze a concrete bureaucracy in action; his successors initially looked at bureaucracy (generalized today into the study of organization) in the formal categories of Weber. Gradually there emerged a concern with "informal organization," the nonblueprinted operations of organization. Because of the restricted use of the term "informal organization" to refer to behavior unplanned by top-level officials, there has been inadequate attention to bureaucracy as an on-going system involving the interaction of individuals and groups with complex (and frequently competing) pressures and motivations. Recently, Alvin Gouldner and Peter Blau, influenced by Weber and Merton, have attempted to apply this fuller approach to the study of organization, which is one of the most promising fields in contemporary sociology. Gouldner's emphasis on differentiating various types of bureaucracies and studying their effects is one of the most important steps forward from Weber's description of the ideal-type form of bureaucracy.

Weber's work obviously touches on the prospects of democratic and responsible forms of government. He saw a need for charismatic qualities in a leader to win and maintain mass support; a legal framework and supporting norms are necessary to give a role to parliament and to prevent a seizure of power by illegal means.

A staunch German patriot, Weber was a severe and outspoken critic of Kaiser Wilhelm II both before and during World War I. He saw the Kaiser as a political dilettante, neither providing secure leadership or permitting "real politicians" to govern. Politics to Weber was a high and demanding calling in a perilous world. He asserted that only political infants believed that good came only from good and evil from evil. The necessity for decision and for the courage to be a politician arose from the responsibility of assaying means and ends, choosing a line of action and resolutely bearing the weight of the outcome.

His view was gloomy for he saw ahead a "polar night of icy darkness and hardness." His mode of accommodation was through passion and detachment—the passion to fight for what one believed in; the detachment to recognize the role of one's values and to attempt to divorce them from the scientific process.

In the last chapter, we have put together comments of Weber on the political scene, especially on that of Germany just before and during World War I. Weber's concerns were for the immediate issues facing Germany; they have, however, a reverberating quality because they confront the values of humanity, science, and politics, especially the dangers of bureaucratic absolutism.

We can be confident that Weber's work will continue to have great importance in social science. The problems that he selected and the acuity of his vision make his writings germane to the issues of industrialized society. Utilizing his writings as a "living document" rather than as a revered and fixed treasure will enrich the work of his successors. We are all post-Weberians now.

1

Basic Concepts of Sociology*

Section 1. The word "sociology" is used in many different senses. In our context it shall mean that science which aims at the interpretative understanding of social conduct and thus at the explanation of its causes, its course, and its effects. Human behavior shall be called "conduct" (*Handeln*) when, and in so far as, the person or persons acting combine with their behavior some subjective meaning. The behavior may be mental or external; it may consist in action or in omission to act. Conduct will be called "social conduct" where its intention is related by the actor or actors to the conduct of others and oriented accordingly in its course.

. . . . .

Section 2. Like any other conduct, social conduct may be determined in any one of the following four ways:

It may, first, be determined rationally and oriented toward an end. In that case it is determined by the expectation that objects in the world outside or other human beings will behave in a certain way, and by the use of such expectations as conditions of, or as means toward, the achievement of the actor's own, rationally desired and considered, aims. This case will be called *purpose-rational* conduct (*zweckrational*).

Or, social conduct may be determined, second, by the conscious faith in the absolute worth of the conduct as such, independent of

---

* Reprinted by permission of the publishers from *Max Weber on Law in Economy and Society*, edited and annotated by Max Rheinstein (Cambridge, Mass.: Harvard University Press, 1954), pp. 1–10. Copyright, 1954, by The President and Fellows of Harvard College. It is a translation of part of the first chapter of Part I of *Wirtschaft und Gesellschaft*. The entire part is available in *The Theory of Social and Economic Organization*, ed. Talcott Parsons (New York: The Free Press of Glencoe, Inc., 1947).

any aim, and measured by some such standard as ethics, aesthetics, or religion. This case will be called *value-rational* conduct (*wert-rational*).

Or, third, social conduct may be determined *affectually*, especially *emotionally*, by actual constellations of feelings and emotions.

Or, it may, fourth, be determined *traditionalistically*.

. . . . .

Section 3. The term "social relationship" will be used to mean the case where two or more persons are engaged in conduct the meaning of which is directed and thus oriented from one person to the other. Hence a social relationship simply consists in the probability that human beings will act in some (sensibly) determinable way; it is completely irrelevant why such a probability exists. Where it exists there is a social relationship, and absolutely no more is required for its existence.

. . . . .

Section 4. Within the realm of social conduct one finds factual regularities, that is, courses of action which, with a typically identical meaning, are repeated by the actors or simultaneously occur among numerous actors. It is with such *types* of conduct that sociology is concerned, in contrast to history, which is interested in the causal connections of important, i.e., fateful, *single* events.

An actually existing probability of a *regularity* of an orientation of social conduct will be called "usage" (*Brauch*) where, and in so far as, the probability of its existence within a group of people is based on *nothing but actual habit* (*Übung*). A usage will be called a "custom" if the actual habit is based upon long standing. Where, on the other hand, a usage is determined *exclusively* by the fact that all the actors' conduct is *aim-rationally* oriented toward identical expectations, it will be called a "usage determined by the interest situation."

Fashion constitutes a special case of usage. In contrast to custom we shall speak of fashion where the conduct in question is motivated by its *novelty* rather than long standing as in the case of custom.

. . . . .

In contrast to "convention" and "law" we shall speak of "custom" where the rule is not externally guaranteed but where the actor conforms to it "without thinking" or for such reasons as simple convenience, and where others belonging to the same group of people can be expected to act in the same way for the same reasons. In this meaning custom thus does not claim any "validity"; nobody is in any

way required to abide by it. However, the transition from this case
to those of convention or law is indefinite. Factual custom everywhere
has begotten a feeling of oughtness. At present it is a custom that in
the morning we eat a breakfast of some definable content. However,
nobody (except a hotel guest) "ought" to do so. Besides, the custom
has not prevailed at all times. On the other hand, the ways in which
we dress are, today at least, no longer mere custom. They have become
convention.

. . . . .

Section 5. Conduct, especially social conduct, and quite particularly a social relationship, can be oriented on the part of the actors
toward their *idea* (*Vorstellung*) of the existence of a *legitimate order*.
The probability of such an orientation shall be called the *validity* of
the order in question.

1. "Validity" of an order is thus to mean more than the mere regularity of the course of social conduct as determined by custom or
interest situations. The fact that movers regularly advertise near the
dates people are moving from one apartment to another is caused
exclusively by their interest situation. The fact that a salesman regularly visits a certain customer on a certain day of the week or month
is either habit of long standing or also caused by his interests (he
may follow a regular turn). But the fact that a public officer shows
up at his office every day at the same hour is determined not only by
routine (custom) or his interest situation but regularly also by the
validity of an order (viz., the civil service rules) as a command the
violation of which will not only involve detriments but will also, at
least normally, be abhorrent to his sense of duty in the value-rational
manner.

2. Only then will the content of a social relationship be called a
social order if the conduct is, approximately and on the average,
oriented toward determinable "maxims." Only then will an order be
called "valid" if the orientation toward those maxims occurs, among
other reasons, also because it is in some appreciable way regarded by
the actor as in some way obligatory or exemplary for him. In actual
life, conduct may be oriented toward an order for a great variety of
motives. But the fact that, among other motives, the order appears
to at least some of the actors as exemplary or obligatory and thus as
binding, increases, often considerably, the probability that conduct
will really be oriented toward the order. An order which is obeyed
for the sole reason of aim-rationality is generally less stable than con-

duct which, because of its long standing, is oriented toward a custom. Indeed, that latter attitude is the much more frequent. But even more stable is the conduct oriented toward a custom which is endowed with the prestige of exemplariness or obligatoriness or, in other words, of "legitimacy." But, of course, the transitions from the orientation of conduct toward an order by virtue of mere tradition or mere aim-rationality to the belief in legitimacy are indeterminate in actual life.

3. There can be orientation toward an order even where its meaning (as generally understood) is not necessarily obeyed. The probability that the order be to some extent valid (as an obligatory norm) can also occur where its meaning is "evaded" or "violated." Such orientation may be of a merely aim-rational kind: The thief orients his conduct toward the validity of the criminal law, viz., by trying to conceal it. The very fact that the order is valid within a group of people makes it necessary for him to conceal its violation. This case is, of course, marginal. Very frequently the order is violated only in one or another partial respect, or its violation is sought to be passed off as legitimate, with a varying measure of good faith. Or several different interpretations of the meaning of the order coexist alongside each other. In that case the sociologist will regard each one as valid in exactly so far as it is actually determinative of conduct. It is, indeed, in no way difficult for the sociologist to recognize that several, possibly mutually contradictory, orders are valid within the same group. Even one and the same individual may orient his conduct toward mutually contradictory orders. He can do so successively; such cases can, indeed, be observed all the time; but orientation of conduct toward mutually contradictory orders can occur with respect to one and the same conduct. One who engages in a duel orients his conduct toward the honor code; but he also orients it toward the criminal law [by which duelling is prohibited] by keeping the duel secret or, in the opposite manner, by voluntarily appearing in court. Where, however, evasion or violation of the order (i.e., of the meaning generally ascribed to it) has become the rule, the order has come to be valid in but a limited sense or has ceased to be valid altogether. For the lawyer an order is either valid or not; but no such alternative exists for the sociologist. Fluid transitions exist between validity and non-validity, and mutually contradictory orders can be valid alongside each other. Each one is valid simply in proportion to the probability that conduct will actually be oriented toward it.

.   .   .   .   .

Section 6. The legitimacy of an order can be *guaranteed* in several ways:

I. It may be guaranteed purely *subjectively* and such subjective guarantee may be either

1. merely affectual, i.e., through emotional surrender; or

2. value-rational, i.e., determined by the faith in the absolute validity of the order as the expression of ultimate, binding values of an ethical, aesthetical, or other kind; or

3. religious, i.e., determined by the belief that salvation depends upon obedience to the order.

II. The legitimacy of an order may, however, be guaranteed also by the expectation of certain external effects, i.e., by interest situations.

An order will be called *convention* where its validity is externally guaranteed by the probability that a violation will meet with the (relatively) general and practically significant *disapproval* of a determinable group of people.

An order will be called *law* if it is externally guaranteed by the probability that coercion (physical or psychological), to bring about conformity or avenge violation, will be applied by a *staff* of people holding themselves specially ready for that purpose.

1. Under *convention* we shall thus understand that *custom* which, within a given group, is approved as "valid" and guaranteed against deviation by disapproval. It differs from "law," as defined here, by the absence of a *staff* holding itself ready to use coercion. Stammler's distinction of convention from law according to whether or not submission is "voluntary," neither corresponds to common linguistic usage nor does it fit his own illustrations. Everybody is seriously expected and regarded as obliged to conform to such conventions as those of the usual modes of salutation, of decent dress, or of the general modes of social intercourse. Conformance to such conventions is in no way so voluntary as, for example, the choice of the manner of cooking. A violation of convention, especially in the frame of so-called professional ethics, often meets with most effective and serious retribution in the form of social boycott by the members of the profession, a retribution which may be more effective than any legal coercion. Nothing is lacking but the staff which could hold itself specifically ready for action meant to guarantee obedience, such as judges, prosecutors, policemen, or sheriffs. Again, however, there is no clear-cut dividing line. There is a marginal case, consisting in the formally threatened and *organized* boycott. In our terminology this

already constitutes a means of legal coercion. It is irrelevant in the present context that in certain cases a convention may, in addition to general disapproval, be protected by other means. An illustration of this situation is presented by the case of the visitor who refuses to leave another's house when asked to do so. He violates a convention; but the master of the house may also expel him bodily. In such a case coercion is applied not by a special staff, but by some particular individual who is able to do so just in consequence of the general disapproval of the violation of the convention.

2. In our context the concept of law will be defined as an order which depends upon an enforcement *staff*. In other connections different definitions may well be appropriate. The enforcement staff does, of course, not necessarily have to be of the kind we know today. It is unnecessary, in particular, that there be any *judicial* organ. In the case of blood vengeance and feud the enforcement staff consists in the clan, provided that its reaction is actually determined by some kind of regulatory order. We must recognize, however, that this case represents the very limit of what can still be regarded as "legal coercion." Time and again international law has been said not to be "law," because it lacks a supra-national enforcement agency. Indeed, our definition of law, too, would not apply to an order which is guaranteed merely by the expectation of disapproval and reprisals on the part of those who are harmed by its violation, i.e., merely by convention and self-interest rather than by a staff of persons whose conduct is *specially* oriented toward the observation of the regulatory order. Yet, legal terminology may be quite different.

Irrelevant, too, are the means of coercion. The friendly "admonition," as it could be found in some sects as the first degree of mild coercion of the sinner, constitutes coercion in our sense, provided it is regulated by some order and applied by a staff. The same is to be said about the censorial "reprimand" as a means to guarantee the observance of "ethical" duties and, even more so, about psychological coercion through ecclesiastical discipline. Hence "law" may be guaranteed by hierocratic authority just as it may be guaranteed politically, or through the statute of an association, or domestic authority, or through a sodality or some other association. The [peculiar] rules of [German students' fraternities, known as] the *comment* [and regulating such matters as convivial drinking or singing] are also "law" in our sense, just as the case of those [legally regulated but unenforceable] duties which are mentioned in Section 888, par. 2 of the [German] Code of Civil Procedure [for instance, the duty arising from an engagement to marry].

Not every valid order is necessarily of an abstract, general character. Nowadays we strictly distinguish between the general "norm of law" and the concrete "judicial decision." Such a distinction was not made at all times. An "order" may thus consist in the ordering of one single concrete situation.

. . . . .

An "externally" guaranteed order may also be guaranteed "internally." The relationship between law, convention, and ethics does not present any problem to the sociologist. To him an "ethical" standard is one which applies to human conduct that specific kind of evaluating *faith* which claims to determine what is "ethically good," just as any conduct which claims to be "beautiful," by so doing, subjects itself to the standard of aesthetics. Normative ideas of this kind can have a powerful influence upon conduct even though they may lack any external guarantee. External guaranties will be usually lacking where the violation of the standard does not appreciably affect the interests of others. On the other hand, they are frequently guaranteed religiously. Possibly, they may also be guaranteed by convention (in our sense of the term), i.e., through disapproval or boycott; in addition, there may be the legal guaranty through the police or the means of criminal or private law. "Ethics," which is valid in the sociological sense, usually is guaranteed by convention, i.e., by the probability of its violation meeting with disapproval. Not every conventionally or legally guaranteed norm, however, claims also to be one of ethics. Legal norms are frequently motivated by mere expediency and thus claim ethical character even less than the norms of convention. Whether or not a normative idea which is actually held by human beings belongs to the realm of ethics or, in other words, whether or not a given norm is one of "mere" law or convention must be decided *by the sociologist* exclusively in accordance with that notion of the "ethical" which is actually held by the people in question. It is not possible, however, to state any general propositions in this respect.

. . . . .

Section 7. The actors can ascribe legitimate validity to an order in a variety of ways.

The order can be recognized as legitimate, first, by virtue of tradition: valid is that which has always been.

Second, the order may be treated as legitimate by virtue of affectual, especially emotional, faith; this situation occurs especially in the case of the newly revealed or the exemplary.

Third, the order may be treated as legitimate by virtue of value-rational faith: valid is that which has been deduced as absolutely demanded.

Fourth, legitimacy can be ascribed to an order by virtue of positive enactment of recognized *legality.*

Such legality can be regarded as legitimate either (a) because the enactment has been agreed upon by all those who are concerned; or (b) by virtue of imposition by a domination of human beings over human beings which is treated as legitimate and meets with acquiescence.

The details will be discussed in the chapters dealing with the sociology of domination and of law. At present the following brief remarks will suffice.

(1) The oldest and most universally found type of validity of orders is that which is based upon the sacredness of tradition. The psychological blocks to any change of an inveterate usage are strengthened by the apprehension of magical detriments. An order which has once become valid is furthermore perpetuated by those manifold interests which arise with respect to the continuation of acquiescence in its existence.

(2) In early society, down to the statutes of the Hellenic *aisymnetes,* conscious creation of new orders appeared almost exclusively as prophetic oracle or at least as revelation enjoying prophetical sanction and thus held sacred. Acquiescence thus depended upon the faith in the legitimacy of the prophet. In periods of strict traditionalism no new order could thus arise without new revelation unless the new order was not looked upon as such but was regarded as a truth that had already been valid although it had been temporarily obscured and had thus been in need of rediscovery.

(3) The purest type of value-rational validity is represented by natural law. The influence of its logically deduced propositions upon actual conduct may lag far behind their theoretical claims; that they have had some influence cannot be denied, however. Its propositions must be distinguished from those of revealed, of enacted, and of traditional law.

(4) Today the most common form of legitimacy is the belief in legality, i.e., the acquiescence in enactments which are formally correct and which have been made in the accustomed manner. The

contrast between agreed and imposed enactments is not an absolute one. In the past it was often necessary for an order to be agreed upon unanimously if it was to be treated as legitimate. Today, however, it frequently happens that an order is agreed upon only by a majority of the members of the group in question, with the acquiescence, however, of those who hold different opinions. In such cases the order is actually imposed by the majority upon the minority. Very frequent also is the case that a violent, or ruthless, or simply energetic minority imposes an order which is also regarded as legitimate by those who were originally opposed. Where voting is the legal method of creating or changing an order, it happens very often that a minority achieves formal majority, but with the acquiescence of the actual majority, so that majority rule is a mere appearance.

The faith in the legality of an agreed order can be traced to fairly early periods and can also be found among so-called primitive peoples; almost always is it supplemented, however, in such cases, by the authority of oracles.

(5) Acquiescence in an imposed order, in so far as it does not depend upon mere fear or upon considerations of purpose-rationality, presupposes the belief that the power of domination of him or those by whom the order is imposed is in some sense legitimate. This phenomenon will be discussed *infra*.

(6) Unless the order is an entirely new one, acquiescence in it is generally based upon a combination of considerations of self-interest, of tradition, and of belief in legality. Very often those who thus acquiesce are in no way aware of whether the case is one of custom, convention, or law. It is then the sociologist's task to find out which kind of validity is the typical one.

. . . . .

Section 8. A social relationship will be called *struggle* in so far as the conduct of a party is oriented toward the intention of making his own will prevail against the resistance of the other party or parties. Such means of struggle as do not consist in actual physical violence shall be called *peaceful means of struggle*. The peaceful struggle will be called *competition* if it is carried on as formally peaceful endeavor to obtain the power of disposition over opportunities which are coveted also by others.

2

The Ideal-type*

We have in abstract economic theory an illustration of those synthetic constructs which have been designated as "*ideas*" of historical phenomena. It offers us an ideal picture of events on the commodity-market under conditions of a society organized on the principles of an exchange economy, free competition and rigorously rational conduct. This conceptual pattern brings together certain relationships and events of historical life into a complex, which is conceived as an internally consistent system. Substantively, this construct in itself is like a *utopia* which has been arrived at by the analytical accentuation of certain elements of reality. Its relationship to the empirical data consists solely in the fact that where market-conditioned relationships of the type referred to by the abstract construct are discovered or suspected to exist in reality to some extent, we can make the *characteristic* features of this relationship pragmatically *clear* and *understandable* by reference to an *ideal-type*. This procedure can be indispensable for heuristic as well as expository purposes. The ideal typical concept will help to develop our skill in imputation in *research*: it *is* no "hypothesis" but it offers guidance to the construction of hypotheses. It is not a *description* of reality but it aims to give unambiguous means of expression to such a description. It is thus the "idea" of the *historically* given modern society, based on an exchange economy, which is developed for us by quite the same logical principles as are used in constructing the idea of the medieval "city

* From *The Methodology of the Social Sciences*, ed. Edward A. Shils and Henry A. Finch (New York: The Free Press of Glencoe, Inc., 1949), pp. 89–92, 93–94, 97–99. The essay of which it is a part is entitled " 'Objectivity' in Social Science and Social Policy" and was first published in 1904 in the *Archiv für Sozialwissenschaft und Sozialpolitik*, of which Weber had recently become an editor.

economy" as a "genetic" concept. When we do this, we construct the concept "city economy" not as an average of the economic structures actually existing in all the cities observed but as an *ideal-type*. An ideal type is formed by the one-sided *accentuation* of one or more points of view and by the synthesis of a great many diffuse, discrete, more or less present and occasionally absent *concrete individual* phenomena, which are arranged according to those one-sidedly emphasized viewpoints into a unified *analytical* construct (*Gedankenbild*). In its conceptual purity, this mental construct (*Gedankenbild*) cannot be found empirically anywhere in reality. It is a *utopia*. Historical research faces the task of determining in each individual case, the extent to which this ideal-construct approximates to or diverges from reality, to what extent for example, the economic structure of a certain city is to be classified as a "city-economy." When carefully applied, those concepts are particularly useful in research and exposition. In very much the same way one can work the "idea" of "handicraft" into a utopia by arranging certain traits, actually found in an unclear, confused state in the industrial enterprises of the most diverse epochs and countries, into a consistent ideal-construct by an accentuation of their essential tendencies. This ideal-type is then related to the idea (*Gedankenausdruck*) which one finds expressed there. One can further delineate a society in which all branches of economic and even intellectual activity are governed by maxims which appear to be applications of the same principle which characterizes the ideal-typical "handicraft" system. Furthermore, one can juxtapose alongside the ideal typical "handicraft" system the antithesis of a correspondingly ideal-typical capitalistic productive system, which has been abstracted out of certain features of modern large scale industry. On the basis of this, one can delineate the utopia of a "capitalistic" culture, i.e., one in which the governing principle is the investment of private capital. This procedure would accentuate certain individual concretely diverse traits of modern material and intellectual culture in its unique aspects into an ideal construct which from our point of view would be completely self-consistent. This would then be the delineation of an *"idea"* of *capitalistic culture*. We must disregard for the moment whether and how this procedure could be carried out. It is possible, or rather, it must be accepted as certain that numerous, indeed a very great many, utopias of this sort can be worked out, of which *none* is like another, and *none* of which can be observed in empirical reality as an actually existing economic system, but each of which however claims that it is a representation of the "idea" of capitalistic culture. Each of these can claim to be a representation of the "idea" of capitalistic culture to the extent that it has really taken certain traits, meaningful in their essential features, from the empirical reality of our culture and brought them together into a unified ideal-construct. For those phenomena which interest us as cultural phenomena are interesting to us with respect to very different kinds of evaluative ideas to which we relate them. Inasmuch as the "points of view" from which they can become significant for us are very diverse, the most varied criteria can be applied to the selection of the traits which are to enter into the construction of an ideal-typical view of a particular culture.

What is the significance of such ideal-typical constructs for an empirical science, as we wish to constitute it? Before going any further, we should emphasize that the idea of an ethical *imperative*, of a "model" of what "ought" to exist is to be carefully distinguished from the analytical construct, which is "ideal" in the strictly logical sense of the term. It is a matter here of constructing relationships which our imagination accepts as plausibly motivated and hence as "objectively possible" and which appear as *adequate* from the nomological standpoint.

・　・　・　・　・

. . . the ideal-type is an attempt to analyze historically unique configurations or their individual components by means of genetic concepts. Let us take for instance the concepts "church" and "sect." They may be broken down purely classificatorily into complexes of characteristics whereby not only the distinction between them but also the content of the concept must constantly remain fluid. If however I wish to formulate the concept of "sect" genetically, e.g., with reference to certain important cultural significances which the "sectarian spirit" has had for modern culture, certain characteristics of both become *essential* because they stand in an adequate causal relationship to those influences. However, the concepts thereupon become ideal-typical in the sense that they appear in full conceptual *integrity* either not at all or only in individual instances. Here as elsewhere every concept which is not purely classificatory diverges from reality. But the discursive nature of our knowledge, i.e., the fact that we comprehend reality only through a chain of intellectual modifications postulates such a conceptual shorthand. Our imagination can often dispense with explicit conceptual formulations as a means of *investigation*. But as regards exposition, to the extent that it wishes to be unambiguous, the use of precise formulations in the sphere of cultural analysis is in many cases absolutely necessary. Whoever disregards it entirely must confine himself to the formal aspect of cultural phenomena, e.g., to legal history. The universe of legal norms is naturally clearly definable and is valid (in the *legal* sense!) for historical reality. But social science in our sense is concerned with practical *significance*. This significance however can very often be brought unambiguously to mind only by relating the empirical data to an ideal limiting case. If the historian (in the widest sense of the word) rejects an attempt to construct such ideal types as a "theoretical construction," i.e., as useless or dispensable for his concrete heuristic purposes, the inevitable consequence is either that he consciously or unconsciously uses other similar concepts without formulating them verbally and elaborating them logically or that he remains stuck in the realm of the vaguely "felt."

Nothing, however, is more dangerous than the *confusion* of theory and history stemming from naturalistic prejudices. This confusion expresses itself firstly in the belief that the "true" content and the essence of historical reality is portrayed in such theoretical constructs or secondly, in the use of these constructs as a procrustean bed into which history is to be forced or thirdly, in the hypostatization of such "ideas" as real "forces" and as a "true" reality which operates behind the passage of events and which works itself out in history.

· · · · ·

There is still another even more complicated significance implicit in such ideal-typical presentations. They regularly seek to be, or are unconsciously, ideal-types not only in the *logical* sense but also in the *practical* sense, i.e., they are *model types* which—in our illustration—contain what, from the point of view of the expositor, *should* be and what *to him* is "essential" in Christianity *because it is enduringly valuable*. If this is consciously or—as it is more frequently—unconsciously the case, they contain ideals *to* which the expositor *evaluatively* relates Christianity. These ideals are tasks and ends towards which he orients his "idea" of Christianity and which naturally can and indeed doubtless always will differ greatly from the values which other persons, for instance, the early Christians, connected with Christianity. In this sense, however, the "ideas" are naturally no longer purely *logical* auxiliary devices, no longer concepts with which reality is compared, but ideals by which it is evaluatively *judged*.

Here it is no longer a matter of the purely theoretical procedure of treating empirical reality with respect to values but of value-judgments which are integrated into the concept of "Christianity." Because the ideal type claims empirical validity here, it penetrates into the realm of the evaluative interpretation of Christianity. The sphere of empirical science has been left behind and we are confronted with a profession of faith, not an ideal-typical construct. As fundamental as this distinction is in principle, the confusion of these two basically different meanings of the term "idea" appears with extraordinary frequency in historical writings. It is always close at hand whenever the descriptive historian begins to develop his "conception" of a personality or an epoch. In contrast with the fixed ethical standards which Schlosser applied in the spirit of rationalism, the modern relativistically educated historian who on the one hand seeks to "understand" the epoch of which he speaks "in its own terms," and on the other still seeks to "judge" it, feels the need to derive the standards for his judgment from the subject-matter itself, i.e., to allow the "idea" in the sense of the ideal to emerge from the "idea" in the sense of the "ideal-type." The esthetic satisfaction produced by such a procedure constantly tempts him to disregard the line where these two ideal types diverge—an error which on the one hand hampers the value-judgment and on the other, strives to free itself from the responsibility for its own judgment. In contrast with this, the elementary duty of scientific self-control and the only way to avoid serious and foolish blunders requires a sharp, precise distinction between the logically comparative analysis of reality by ideal-types in the logical sense and the value-judgment of reality on the basis of ideals. An "ideal type" in our sense, to repeat once more, has no connection at all with value-judgments, and it has nothing to do with any type of perfection other than a purely logical one. There are ideal types of brothels as well as of religions; there are also ideal types of those kinds of brothels which are technically "expedient" from the point of view of police ethics as well as those of which the exact opposite is the case.

3

The Protestant Ethic*

The impulse to acquisition, pursuit of gain, of money, of the greatest possible amount of money, has in itself nothing to do with capitalism. This impulse exists and has existed among waiters, physicians, coachmen, artists, prostitutes, dishonest officials, soldiers, nobles, crusaders, gamblers, and beggars. One may say that it has been common to all sorts and conditions of men at all times and in all countries of the earth, wherever the objective possibility of it is or has been given. It should be taught in the kindergarten of cultural history that this naïve idea of capitalism must be given up once and for all. Unlimited greed for gain is not in the least identical with capitalism, and is still less its spirit. Capitalism may even be identical with the restraint, or at least a rational tempering, of this irrational impulse. But capitalism is identical with the pursuit of profit, and forever renewed profit, by means of continuous, rational, capitalistic enterprise. For it must be so: in a wholly capitalistic order of society, an individual capitalistic enterprise which did not take advantage of its opportunities for profit-making would be doomed to extinction. [p. 1]

Hence in a universal history of culture the central problem for us is not, in the last analysis, even from a purely economic view-point, the development of capitalistic activity as such, differing in different cultures only in form: the adventurer type, or capitalism in trade, war, politics, or administration as sources of gain. It is rather the origin of this sober bourgeois capitalism with its rational organization

* Extracts from *The Protestant Ethic and the Spirit of Capitalism*, by Max Weber, trans. Talcott Parsons (New York: Charles Scribner's Sons, 1958), are used by permission of Charles Scribner's Sons and George Allen & Unwin, Ltd. This chapter should be read in conjunction with the following one on China.

of free labour. Or in terms of cultural history, the problem is that of the origin of the Western bourgeois class and of its peculiarities, a problem which is certainly closely connected with that of the origin of the capitalistic organization of labour, but is not quite the same thing. For the bourgeois as a class existed prior to the development of the peculiar modern form of capitalism, though, it is true, only in the Western hemisphere. [pp. 23-24]

. . . it is a question of the specific and peculiar rationalism of Western culture. Now by this term very different things may be understood, as the following discussion will repeatedly show. There is, for example, rationalization of mystical contemplation, that is of an attitude which, viewed from other departments of life, is specifically irrational, just as much as there are rationalizations of economic life, of technique, of scientific research, of military training, of law and administration. Furthermore, each one of these fields may be rationalized in terms of very different ultimate values and ends, and what is rational from one point of view may well be irrational from another. Hence rationalizations of the most varied character have existed in various departments of life and in all areas of culture. To characterize their differences from the view-point of cultural history it is necessary to know what departments are rationalized, and in what direction. It is hence our first concern to work out and to explain genetically the special peculiarity of Occidental rationalism, and within this field that of the modern Occidental form. Every such attempt at explanation must, recognizing the fundamental importance of the economic factor, above all take account of the economic conditions. But at the same time the opposite correlation must not be left out of consideration. For though the development of economic rationalism is partly dependent on rational technique and law, it is at the same time determined by the ability and disposition of men to adopt certain types of practical rational conduct. When these types have been obstructed by spiritual obstacles, the development of rational economic conduct has also met serious inner resistance. The magical and religious forces, and the ethical ideas of duty based upon them, have in the past always been among the most important formative influences on conduct. In the studies collected here we shall be concerned with these forces. [pp. 26-27]

The most important opponent with which the spirit of capitalism, in the sense of a definite standard of life claiming ethical sanction, has had to struggle, was that type of attitude and reaction to new situations which we may designate as traditionalism. [pp. 58–59]

. . . we provisionally use the expression spirit of (modern) capitalism to describe that attitude which seeks profit rationally and systematically in the manner which we have illustrated by the example of Benjamin Franklin. This, however, is justified by the historical fact that that attitude of mind has on the one hand found its most suitable expression in capitalistic enterprise, while on the other the enterprise has derived its most suitable motive force from the spirit of capitalism. [pp. 64–65]

The ideal type of the capitalistic entrepreneur . . . has no relation to . . . [social] climbers. He avoids ostentation and unnecessary expenditure, as well as conscious enjoyment of his power, and is embarrassed by the outward signs of the social recognition which he receives. His manner of life is, in other words, often, and we shall have to investigate the historical significance of just this important fact, distinguished by a certain ascetic tendency, as appears clearly enough in the sermon of Franklin which we have quoted. It is, namely, by no means exceptional, but rather the rule, for him to have a sort of modesty which is essentially more honest than the reserve which Franklin so shrewdly recommends. He gets nothing out of his wealth for himself, except the irrational sense of having done his job well.

But it is just that which seems to the pre-capitalistic man so incomprehensible and mysterious, so unworthy and contemptible. That anyone should be able to make it the sole purpose of his life-work, to sink into the grave weighed down with a great material load of money and goods, seems to him explicable only as the product of a perverse instinct, the auri sacra fames. [pp. 71–72]

Now, how could activity, which was at best ethically tolerated, turn into a calling in the sense of Benjamin Franklin? The fact to be explained historically is that in the most highly capitalistic centre of that time, in Florence of the fourteenth and fifteenth centuries, the money and capital market of all the great political Powers, this attitude was considered ethically unjustifiable, or at best to be tolerated. But in the backwoods small bourgeois circumstances of Pennsylvania in the eighteenth century, where business threatened for simple lack of money to fall back into barter, where there was hardly a sign of large enterprise, where only the earliest beginnings of banking were to be found, the same thing was considered the essence of moral conduct, even commanded in the name of duty. To speak here of a reflection of material conditions in the ideal superstructure would be patent nonsense. What was the background of ideas which could account for the sort of activity apparently directed toward profit alone as a calling toward which the individual feels himself to have an ethical obligation? For it was this idea which gave the way of life of the new entrepreneur its ethical foundation and justification. [pp. 74–75]

The religious believer can make himself sure of his state of grace either in that he feels himself to be the vessel of the Holy Spirit or the tool of the divine will. In the former case his religious life tends to mysticism and emotionalism, in the latter to ascetic action; Luther stood close to the former type, Calvinism belonged definitely to the latter. The Calvinist also wanted to be saved *sola fide*. But since Calvin viewed all pure feelings and emotions, no matter how exalted they might seem to be, with suspicion, faith had to be proved by its objective results in order to provide a firm foundation for the *certitudo salutis*. It must be a *fides efficax*, the call to salvation an effectual calling (expression used in Savoy Declaration).

If we now ask further, by what fruits the Calvinist thought himself able to identify true faith? the answer is: by a type of Christian conduct which served to increase the glory of God. Just what does so serve is to be seen in his own will as revealed either directly through the Bible or indirectly through the purposeful order of the world which he has created (*lex naturæ*). Especially by comparing the condition of one's own soul with that of the elect, for instance the patriarchs, according to the Bible, could the state of one's own grace be known. Only one of the elect really has the *fides efficax*, only he is able by virtue of his rebirth (*regeneratio*) and the resulting sanctification (*sanctificatio*) of his whole life, to augment the glory of God by real, and not merely apparent, good works. It was through the consciousness that his conduct, at least in its fundamental character and constant ideal (*propositum obœdientiæ*), rested on a power within himself working for the glory of God; that it is not only willed of God but rather done by God that he attained the highest good towards which this religion strove, the certainty of salvation. That it was attainable was proved by 2 Cor. xiii. 5. Thus, however useless good works might be as a means of attaining salvation, for even the elect remain beings of the flesh, and everything they do falls infinitely short of divine standards, nevertheless, they are indispensable as a sign of election. They are the technical means, not of purchasing salvation, but of getting rid of the fear of damnation. In this sense they are occasionally referred to as directly necessary for salvation or the *possessio salutis* is made conditional on them.

In practice this means that God helps those who help themselves. Thus the Calvinist, as it is sometimes put, himself creates his own salvation, or, as would be more correct, the conviction of it. But this creation cannot, as in Catholicism, consist in a gradual accumulation of individual good works to one's credit, but rather in a systematic self-control which at every moment stands before the inexorable alternative, chosen or damned. [pp. 113–15]

The God of Calvinism demanded of His believers not single good works, but a life of good works combined into a unified system. There was no place for the very human Catholic cycle of sin, repentance, atonement, release, followed by renewed sin. Nor was there any balance of merit for a life as a whole which could be adjusted by temporal punishments or the Churches' means of grace.

The moral conduct of the average man was thus deprived of its planless and unsystematic character and subjected to a consistent method for conduct as a whole. It is no accident that the name of Methodists stuck to the participants in the last great revival of Puritan ideas in the eighteenth century just as the term Precisians, which has the same meaning, was applied to their spiritual ancestors in the seventeenth century. For only by a fundamental change in the whole meaning of life at every moment and in every action could the effects of grace transforming a man from the *status naturæ* be proved. [pp. 117–18]

. . . In the course of its development Calvinism added . . . the idea of the necessity of proving one's faith in worldly activity. Therein it gave the broader groups of religiously inclined people a positive incentive to asceticism. By founding its ethic in the doctrine of pre-destination, it substituted for the spiritual aristocracy of monks outside of and above the world the spiritual aristocracy of the pre-destined saints of God within the world. It was an aristocracy which, with its character *indelebilis*, was divided from the eternally damned remainder of humanity by a more impassable and in its invisibility more terrifying gulf, than separated the monk of the Middle Ages from the rest of the world about him, a gulf which penetrated all social relations with its sharp brutality. This consciousness of divine grace of the elect and holy was accompanied by an attitude toward the sin of one's neighbour, not of sympathetic understanding based on consciousness of one's own weakness, but of hatred and contempt for him as an enemy of God bearing the signs of eternal damnation. This sort of feeling was capable of such intensity that it sometimes resulted in the formation of sects. This was the case when, as in the Independent movement of the seventeenth century, the genuine Calvinist doctrine that the glory of God required the Church to bring the damned under the law, was outweighed by the conviction that it was an insult to God if an unregenerate soul should be admitted to His house and partake in the sacraments, or even, as a minister, administer them. [pp. 121–22]

As he observed his own conduct, the later Puritan also observed that of God and saw His finger in all the details of life. And, contrary to the strict doctrine of Calvin, he always knew why God took this or that measure. The process of sanctifying life could thus almost take on the character of a business enterprise. A thoroughgoing Christianization of the whole of life was the consequence of this methodical quality of ethical conduct into which Calvinism as distinct from Lutheranism forced men. That this rationality was decisive in its influence on practical life must always be borne in mind in order rightly to understand the influence of Calvinism. On the one hand we can see that it took this element to exercise such an influence at all. But other faiths as well necessarily had a similar influence when their ethical motives were the same in this decisive point, the doctrine of proof. [pp. 124–25]

The fact is that Lutheranism, on account of its doctrine of grace, lacked a psychological sanction of systematic conduct to compel the methodical rationalization of life.

This sanction, which conditions the ascetic character of religion, could doubtless in itself have been furnished by various different religious motives, as we shall soon see. The Calvinistic doctrine of predestination was only one of several possibilities. But nevertheless we have become convinced that in its way it had not only a quite unique consistency, but that its psychological effect was extraordinarily powerful. In comparison with it the non-Calvinistic ascetic movements, considered purely from the view-point of the religious motivation of asceticism, form an attenuation of the inner consistency and power of Calvinism. [p. 128]

One of the fundamental elements of the spirit of modern capitalism, and not only of that but of all modern culture: rational conduct on the basis of the idea of the calling, was born—that is what this discussion has sought to demonstrate—from the spirit of Christian asceticism. One has only to re-read . . . [Benjamin] Franklin . . . in order to see that the essential elements of the attitude which was there called the spirit of capitalism are the same as . . . the content of the Puritan worldly asceticism, only without the religious basis, which by Franklin's time had died away. [p. 180]

. . . Protestant Asceticism was in turn influenced in its development and its character by the totality of social conditions, especially economic. The modern man is in general, even with the best will, unable to give religious ideas a significance for culture and national character which they deserve. But it is, of course, not my aim to substitute for a one-sided materialistic an equally one-sided spiritualistic causal interpretation of culture and of history. Each is equally possible, but each, if it does not serve as the preparation, but as the conclusion of an investigation, accomplishes equally little in the interest of historical truth. [p. 183]

4

Confucianism and Puritanism*

The typical Confucian used his own and his family's savings in order to acquire a literary education and to have himself trained for the examinations. Thus he gained the basis for a cultured status position. The typical Puritan earned plenty, spent little, and reinvested his income as capital in rational capitalist enterprise out of an asceticist compulsion to save. "Rationalism"—and this is our second lesson—was embodied in the spirit of both ethics. But only the Puritan rational ethic with its supra-mundane orientation brought economic rationalism to its consistent conclusion. This happened merely because nothing was further from the conscious Puritan intention. It happened because inner-worldly work was simply expressive of the striving for a transcendental goal. The world, as promised, fell to Puritanism because the Puritans alone "had striven for God and his justice." In this is vested the basic difference between the two kinds of rationalism. Confucian rationalism meant rational adjustment to the world; Puritan rationalism meant rational mastery of the world. Both the Puritan and the Confucian were "sober men." But the rational sobriety of the Puritan was founded in a mighty enthusiasm which the Confucian lacked completely; it was the same enthusiasm which inspired the monk of the Occident. The rejection of the world by occidental asceticism was insolubly linked to its opposite, namely, its eagerness to dominate the world. In the name of a supra-mundane God the imperatives of asceticism were issued to the monk and, in variant and softened form, to the world. Nothing conflicted more with the Confucian ideal of gentility than the idea of a "vocation."

* From *The Religion of China*, ed. Hans Gerth (New York: The Free Press of Glencoe, Inc., 1951), pp. 247–49. This chapter amplifies the argument of *The Protestant Ethic and the Spirit of Capitalism* in a comparative context.

The "princely" man was an aesthetic value; he was not a tool of a god. But the true Christian, the other-worldly and inner-worldly asceticist, wished to be nothing more than a tool of his God; in this he sought his dignity. Since this is what he wished to be he was a useful instrument for rationally transforming and mastering the world.

The Chinese in all probability would be quite capable, probably more capable than the Japanese, of assimilating capitalism which has technically and economically been fully developed in the modern culture area. It is obviously not a question of deeming the Chinese "naturally ungifted" for the demands of capitalism. But compared to the Occident, the varied conditions which externally favored the origin of capitalism in China did not suffice to create it. Likewise capitalism did not originate in occidental or oriental Antiquity, or in India, or where Islamism held sway. Yet in each of these areas different and favorable circumstances seemed to facilitate its rise. Many of the circumstances which could or had to hinder capitalism in China similarly existed in the Occident and assumed definite shape in the period of modern capitalism. Thus, there were the patrimonial traits of occidental rulers, their bureaucracy, and the fact that the money economy was unsettled and undeveloped. The money economy of Ptolemaic Egypt was carried through much more thoroughly than it was in fifteenth or sixteenth century Europe. Circumstances which are usually considered to have been obstacles to capitalist development in the Occident had not existed for thousands of years in China. Such circumstances as the fetters of feudalism, landlordism and, in part also, the guild system were lacking there. Besides, a considerable part of the various trade-restricting monopolies which were characteristic of the Occident did not apparently exist in China. Also, in the past, China knew time and again the political conditions arising out of preparation for war and warfare between competing states. In ancient Babylon and in Antiquity, there were conditions conducive to the rise of political capitalism which the modern period also shares with the past. It might be thought that modern capitalism, interested in free trading opportunity, could have gained ground once the accumulation of wealth and profit from political sources became impossible. This is perhaps comparable to the way in which, in recent times, North America has offered the freest space for the development of high capitalism in the almost complete absence of organization for war.

Political capitalism was common to occidental Antiquity until the time of the Roman emperors, to the Middle Ages, and to the Orient. The pacification of the Empire explains, at least indirectly, the non-existence of political capitalism but it does not explain the non-existence of modern capitalism in China. To be sure the basic characteristics of the "mentality," in this case the practical attitudes toward the world, were deeply co-determined by political and economic destinies. Yet, in view of their autonomous laws, one can hardly fail to ascribe to these attitudes effects strongly counteractive to capitalist development.

Class, Status, Party*

I. ECONOMICALLY DETERMINED
POWER AND THE SOCIAL ORDER

Law exists when there is a probability that an order will be upheld by a specific staff of men who will use physical or psychical compulsion with the intention of obtaining conformity with the order, or of inflicting sanctions for infringement of it. The structure of every legal order directly influences the distribution of power, economic or otherwise, within its respective community. This is true of all legal orders and not only that of the state. In general, we understand by 'power' the chance of a man or of a number of men to realize their own will in a communal action even against the resistance of others who are participating in the action.

'Economically conditioned' power is not, of course, identical with 'power' as such. On the contrary, the emergence of economic power may be the consequence of power existing on other grounds. Man does not strive for power only in order to enrich himself economically. Power, including economic power, may be valued 'for its own sake.' Very frequently the striving for power is also conditioned by the social 'honor' it entails. Not all power, however, entails social honor: The typical American Boss, as well as the typical big speculator, deliberately relinquishes social honor. Quite generally, 'mere economic' power, and especially 'naked' money power, is by no means a recognized basis of social honor. Nor is power the only basis of social honor.

* From *From Max Weber: Essays in Sociology*, ed. and trans. Hans Gerth and C. Wright Mills (New York: Oxford University Press, Inc., 1946), pp. 180–95. Copyright 1946 by Oxford University Press, Inc. Reprinted by permission. This chapter is translated from *Wirtschaft und Gesellschaft*, Part III, Chapter 4.

Indeed, social honor, or prestige, may even be the basis of political or economic power, and very frequently has been. Power, as well as honor, may be guaranteed by the legal order, but, at least normally, it is not their primary source. The legal order is rather an additional factor that enhances the chance to hold power or honor; but it cannot always secure them.

The way in which social honor is distributed in a community between typical groups participating in this distribution we may call the 'social order.' The social order and the economic order are, of course, similarly related to the 'legal order.' However, the social and the economic order are not identical. The economic order is for us merely the way in which economic goods and services are distributed and used. The social order is of course conditioned by the economic order to a high degree, and in its turn reacts upon it.

Now: 'classes,' 'status groups,' and 'parties' are phenomena of the distribution of power within a community.

II. DETERMINATION OF CLASS-SITUATION BY MARKET-SITUATION

In our terminology, 'classes' are not communities; they merely represent possible, and frequent, bases for communal action. We may speak of a 'class' when (1) a number of people have in common a specific causal component of their life chances, in so far as (2) this component is represented exclusively by economic interests in the possession of goods and opportunities for income, and (3) is represented under the conditions of the commodity or labor markets. [These points refer to 'class situation,' which we may express more briefly as the typical chance for a supply of goods, external living conditions, and personal life experiences, in so far as this chance is determined by the amount and kind of power, or lack of such, to dispose of goods or skills for the sake of income in a given economic order. The term 'class' refers to any group of people that is found in the same class situation.]

It is the most elemental economic fact that the way in which the disposition over material property is distributed among a plurality of people, meeting competitively in the market for the purpose of exchange, in itself creates specific life chances. According to the law of marginal utility this mode of distribution excludes the non-owners from competing for highly valued goods; it favors the owners and, in fact, gives to them a monopoly to acquire such goods. Other things being equal, this mode of distribution monopolizes the opportunities for profitable deals for all those who, provided with goods, do not necessarily have to exchange them. It increases, at least generally, their power in price wars with those who, being propertyless, have nothing to offer but their services in native form or goods in a form constituted through their own labor, and who above all are compelled to get rid of these products in order barely to subsist. This mode of distribution gives to the propertied a monopoly on the possibility of transferring property from the sphere of use as a 'fortune,' to the sphere of 'capital goods'; that is, it gives them the entrepreneurial function and all chances to share directly or indirectly in returns on capital. All this holds true within the area in which pure market conditions prevail. 'Property' and 'lack of property' are, therefore, the basic categories of all class situations. It does not matter whether these two categories become effective in price wars or in competitive struggles.

Within these categories, however, class situations are further differentiated: on the one hand, according to the kind of property that is usable for returns; and, on the other hand, according to the kind of services that can be offered in the market. Ownership of domestic buildings; productive establishments; warehouses; stores; agriculturally usable land, large and small holdings—quantitative differences with possibly qualitative consequences—; ownership of mines; cattle; men (slaves); disposition over mobile instruments of production, or capital goods of all sorts, especially money or objects that can be exchanged for money easily and at any time; disposition over products of one's own labor or of others' labor differing according to their various distances from consumability; disposition over transferable monopolies of any kind—all these distinctions differentiate the class situations of the propertied just as does the 'meaning' which they can and do give to the utilization of property, especially to property which has money equivalence. Accordingly, the propertied, for instance, may belong to the class of rentiers or to the class of entrepreneurs.

Those who have no property but who offer services are differentiated just as much according to their kinds of services as according to the way in which they make use of these services, in a continuous or discontinuous relation to a recipient. But always this is the generic connotation of the concept of class: that the kind of chance in the market is the decisive moment which presents a common condition for the individual's fate. 'Class situation' is, in this sense, ultimately 'market situation.' The effect of naked possession *per se*, which among cattle breeders gives the non-owning slave or serf into the power of the cattle owner, is only a forerunner of real 'class' formation. However, in the cattle loan and in the naked severity of the law of debts in such communities, for the first time mere 'possession' as such emerges as decisive for the fate of the individual. This is very much in contrast to the agricultural communities based on labor. The creditor-debtor relation becomes the basis of 'class situations' only in those cities where a 'credit market,' however primitive, with rates of interest increasing according to the extent of dearth and a factual monopolization of credits, is developed by a plutocracy. Therewith 'class struggles' begin.

Those men whose fate is not determined by the chance of using goods or services for themselves on the market, e.g. slaves, are not, however, a 'class' in the technical sense of the term. They are, rather, a 'status group.'

III. COMMUNAL ACTION FLOWING FROM CLASS INTEREST

According to our terminology, the factor that creates 'class' is unambiguously economic interest, and indeed, only those interests involved in the existence of the 'market.' Nevertheless, the concept of 'class-interest' is an ambiguous one: even as an empirical concept it is ambiguous as soon as one understands by it something other than the factual direction of interests following with a certain probability from the class situation for a certain 'average' of those people subjected to the class situation. The class situation and other circumstances remaining the same, the direction in which the individual worker, for instance, is likely to pursue his interests may vary widely, according to whether he is constitutionally qualified for the task at hand to a high, to an average, or to a low degree. In the same way, the direction of interests may vary according to whether or not a *communal* action of a larger or smaller portion of those commonly affected by the 'class situation,' or even an association among them, e.g. a 'trade union,' has grown out of the class situation from which the individual may or may not expect promising results. [Communal action refers to that action which is oriented to the feeling of the actors that they belong together. Societal action, on the other hand, is oriented to a rationally motivated adjustment of interests.] The rise of societal or even of communal action from a common class situation is by no means a universal phenomenon.

The class situation may be restricted in its effects to the generation of essentially *similar* reactions, that is to say, within our terminology, of 'mass actions.' However, it may not have even this result. Furthermore, often merely an amorphous communal action emerges. For example, the 'murmuring' of the workers known in ancient oriental ethics: the moral disapproval of the work-master's conduct, which in its practical significance was probably equivalent to an increasingly typical phenomenon of precisely the latest industrial development, namely, the 'slow down' (the deliberate limiting of work effort) of laborers by virtue of tacit agreement. The degree in which 'communal action' and possibly 'societal action,' emerges from the 'mass actions' of the members of a class is linked to general cultural conditions, especially to those of an intellectual sort. It is also linked to the extent of the contrasts that have already evolved, and is especially linked to the *transparency* of the connections between the causes and the consequences of the 'class situation.' For however different life chances may be, this fact in itself, according to all experience, by no means gives birth to 'class action' (communal action by the members of a class). The fact of being conditioned and the results of the class situation must be distinctly recognizable. For only then the contrast of life chances can be felt not as an absolutely given fact to be accepted, but as a resultant from either (1) the given distribution of property, or (2) the structure of the concrete economic order. It is only then that people may react against the class structure not only through acts of an intermittent and irrational protest, but in the form of rational association. There have been 'class situations' of the first category (1), of a specifically naked and transparent sort, in the urban centers of Antiquity and during the Middle Ages; especially then, when great fortunes were accumulated by factually monopolized trading in industrial products of these localities or in foodstuffs. Furthermore, under certain circumstances, in the rural economy of the most diverse periods, when agriculture was increasingly exploited in a profit-making manner. The most important historical example of the second category (2) is the class situation of the modern 'proletariat.'

IV. TYPES OF 'CLASS STRUGGLE'

Thus every class may be the carrier of any one of the possibly innumerable forms of 'class action,' but this is not necessarily so. In any case, a class does not in itself constitute a community. To treat 'class' conceptually as having the same value as 'community' leads to distortion. That men in the same class situation regularly react in mass actions to such tangible situations as economic ones in the direction of those interests that are most adequate to their average number is an important and after all simple fact for the understanding of historical events. Above all, this fact must not lead to that kind of pseudo-scientific operation with the concepts of 'class' and 'class interests' so frequently found these days, and which has found its most classic expression in the statement of a talented author, that the individual may be in error concerning his interests but that the 'class' is 'infallible' about its interests. Yet, if classes as such are not communities, nevertheless class situations emerge only on the basis of communalization. The communal action that brings forth class situations, however, is not basically action between members of the identical class; it is an action between members of different classes. Communal actions that directly determine the class situation of the worker and the entrepreneur are: the labor market, the commodities market, and the capitalistic enterprise. But, in its turn, the existence of a capitalistic enterprise presupposes that a very specific communal action exists and that it is specifically structured to protect the possession of goods per se, and especially the power of individuals to dispose, in principle freely, over the means of production. The existence of a capitalistic enterprise is preconditioned by a specific kind of 'legal order.' Each kind of class situation, and above all when it rests upon the power of property per se, will become most clearly efficacious when all other determinants of reciprocal relations are, as far as possible, eliminated in their significance. It is in this way that the utilization of the power of property in the market obtains its most sovereign importance.

Now 'status groups' hinder the strict carrying through of the sheer market principle. In the present context they are of interest to us only from this one point of view. Before we briefly consider them, note that not much of a general nature can be said about the more specific kinds of antagonism between 'classes' (in our meaning of the term). The great shift, which has been going on continuously in the past, and up to our times, may be summarized, although at the cost of some precision: the struggle in which class situations are effective has progressively shifted from consumption credit toward, first, competitive struggles in the commodity market and, then, toward price wars on the labor market. The 'class struggles' of antiquity—to the extent that they were genuine class struggles and not struggles between status groups—were initially carried on by indebted peasants, and perhaps also by artisans threatened by debt bondage and struggling against urban creditors. For debt bondage is the normal result of the differentiation of wealth in commercial cities, especially in seaport cities. A similar situation has existed among cattle breeders. Debt relationships as such produced class action up to the time of Cataline. Along with this, and with an increase in provision of grain for the city by transporting it from the outside, the struggle over the means of sustenance emerged. It centered in the first place around the provision of bread and the determination of the price of bread. It lasted throughout antiquity and the entire Middle Ages. The propertyless as such flocked together against those who actually and supposedly were interested in the dearth of bread. This fight spread until it involved all those commodities essential to the way of life and to handicraft production. There were only incipient discussions of wage disputes in antiquity and in the Middle Ages. But they have been slowly increasing up into modern times. In the earlier periods they were completely secondary to slave rebellions as well as to fights in the commodity market.

The propertyless of antiquity and of the Middle Ages protested against monopolies, pre-emption, forestalling, and the withholding of goods from the market in order to raise prices. Today the central issue is the determination of the price of labor.

This transition is represented by the fight for access to the market and for the determination of the price of products. Such fights went on between merchants and workers in the putting-out system of domestic handicraft during the transition to modern times. Since it is quite a general phenomenon we must mention here that the class antagonisms that are conditioned through the market situation are usually most bitter between those who actually and directly participate as opponents in price wars. It is not the rentier, the share-holder, and the banker who suffer the ill will of the worker, but almost exclusively the manufacturer and the business executives who are the direct opponents of workers in price wars. This is so in spite of the fact that it is precisely the cash boxes of the rentier, the share-holder, and the banker into which the more or less 'unearned' gains flow, rather than into the pockets of the manufacturers or of the business executives. This simple state of affairs has very frequently been decisive for the role the class situation has played in the formation of political parties. For example, it has made possible the varieties of patriarchal socialism and the frequent attempts—formerly, at least—of threatened status groups to form alliances with the proletariat against the 'bourgeoisie.'

V. STATUS HONOR

In contrast to classes, *status groups* are normally communities. They are, however, often of an amorphous kind. In contrast to the purely economically determined 'class situation' we wish to designate as 'status situation' every typical component of the life fate of men that is determined by a specific, positive or negative, social estimation of *honor*. This honor may be connected with any quality shared by a plurality, and, of course, it can be knit to a class situation: class distinctions are linked in the most varied ways with status distinctions. Property as such is not always recognized as a status qualification, but in the long run it is, and with extraordinary regularity. In the subsistence economy of the organized neighborhood, very often the richest man is simply the chieftain. However, this often means only an honorific preference. For example, in the so-called pure modern 'democracy,' that is, one devoid of any expressly ordered status privileges for individuals, it may be that only the families coming under approximately the same tax class dance with one another. This example is reported of certain smaller Swiss cities. But status honor need not necessarily be linked with a 'class situation.' On the contrary, it normally stands in sharp opposition to the pretensions of sheer property.

Both propertied and propertyless people can belong to the same status group, and frequently they do with very tangible consequences. This 'equality' of social esteem may, however, in the long run become quite precarious. The 'equality' of status among the American 'gentlemen,' for instance, is expressed by the fact that outside the subordination determined by the different functions of 'business,' it would be

considered strictly repugnant—wherever the old tradition still pre-
vails—if even the richest 'chief,' while playing billiards or cards in
his club in the evening, would not treat his 'clerk' as in every sense
fully his equal in birthright. It would be repugnant if the American
'chief' would bestow upon his 'clerk' the condescending 'benevolence'
marking a distinction of 'position,' which the German chief can never
dissever from his attitude. This is one of the most important reasons
why in America the German 'clubby-ness' has never been able to
attain the attraction that the American clubs have.

VI. GUARANTEES OF STATUS STRATIFICATION

In content, status honor is normally expressed by the fact that
above all else a specific *style of life* can be expected from all those who
wish to belong to the circle. Linked with this expectation are restrictions on 'social' intercourse (that is, intercourse which is not sub-
servient to economic or any other of business's 'functional' purposes).
These restrictions may confine normal marriages to within the status
circle and may lead to complete endogamous closure. As soon as there
is not a mere individual and socially irrelevant imitation of another
style of life, but an agreed-upon communal action of this closing
character, the 'status' development is under way.

In its characteristic form, stratification by 'status groups' on the
basis of conventional styles of life evolves at the present time in the
United States out of the traditional democracy. For example, only
the resident of a certain street ('the street') is considered as belonging to 'society,' is qualified for social intercourse, and is visited and
invited. Above all, this differentiation evolves in such a way as to
make for strict submission to the fashion that is dominant at a given
time in society. This submission to fashion also exists among men in
America to a degree unknown in Germany. Such submission is considered to be an indication of the fact that a given man *pretends* to
qualify as a gentleman. This submission decides, at least *prima facie*,
that he will be treated as such. And this recognition becomes just as
important for his employment chances in 'swank' establishments, and
above all, for social intercourse and marriage with 'esteemed' families, as the qualification for dueling among Germans in the Kaiser's
day. As for the rest: certain families resident for a long time, and, of
course, correspondingly wealthy, e.g. 'F. F. V., i.e. First Families of

Virginia,' or the actual or alleged descendants of the 'Indian Princess' Pocahontas, of the Pilgrim fathers, or of the Knickerbockers, the members of almost inaccessible sects and all sorts of circles setting themselves apart by means of any other characteristics and badges . . . all these elements usurp 'status' honor. The development of status is essentially a question of stratification resting upon usurpation. Such usurpation is the normal origin of almost all status honor. But the road from this purely conventional situation to legal privilege, positive or negative, is easily traveled as soon as a certain stratification of the social order has in fact been 'lived in' and has achieved stability by virtue of a stable distribution of economic power.

VII. 'ETHNIC' SEGREGATION AND 'CASTE'

Where the consequences have been realized to their full extent, the status group evolves into a closed 'caste.' Status distinctions are then guaranteed not merely by conventions and laws, but also by *rituals*. This occurs in such a way that every physical contact with a member of any caste that is considered to be 'lower' by the members of a 'higher' caste is considered as making for a ritualistic impurity and to be a stigma which must be expiated by a religious act. Individual castes develop quite distinct cults and gods.

In general, however, the status structure reaches such extreme consequences only where there are underlying differences which are held to be 'ethnic.' The 'caste' is, indeed, the normal form in which ethnic communities usually live side by side in a 'societalized' manner. These ethnic communities believe in blood relationship and exclude exogamous marriage and social intercourse. Such a caste situation is part of the phenomenon of 'pariah' peoples and is found all over the world. These people form communities, acquire specific occupational traditions of handicrafts or of other arts, and cultivate a belief in their ethnic community. They live in a 'diaspora' strictly segregated from all personal intercourse, except that of an unavoidable sort, and their situation is legally precarious. Yet, by virtue of their economic indispensability, they are tolerated, indeed, frequently privileged, and they live in interspersed political communities. The Jews are the most impressive historical example.

A 'status' segregation grown into a 'caste' differs in its structure from a mere 'ethnic' segregation: the caste structure transforms the horizontal and unconnected coexistences of ethnically segregated groups into a vertical social system of super- and subordination. Correctly formulated: a comprehensive societalization integrates the ethnically divided communities into specific political and communal action. In their consequences they differ precisely in this way: ethnic coexistences condition a mutual repulsion and disdain but allow each ethnic community to consider its own honor as the highest one; the caste structure brings about a social subordination and an acknowledgment of 'more honor' in favor of the privileged caste and status groups. This is due to the fact that in the caste structure ethnic distinctions as such have become 'functional' distinctions within the political societalization (warriors, priests, artisans that are politically important for war and for building, and so on). But even pariah people who are most despised are usually apt to continue cultivating in some manner that which is equally peculiar to ethnic and to status communities: the belief in their own specific 'honor.' This is the case with the Jews.

Only with the negatively privileged status groups does the 'sense of dignity' take a specific deviation. A sense of dignity is the precipitation in individuals of social honor and of conventional demands which a positively privileged status group raises for the deportment of its members. The sense of dignity that characterizes positively privileged status groups is naturally related to their 'being' which does not transcend itself, that is, it is to their 'beauty and excellence' (καλο-κάγαϑια). Their kingdom is 'of this world.' They live for the present and by exploiting their great past. The sense of dignity of the negatively privileged strata naturally refers to a future lying beyond the present, whether it is of this life or of another. In other words, it must be nurtured by the belief in a providential 'mission' and by a belief in a specific honor before God. The 'chosen people's' dignity is nurtured by a belief either that in the beyond 'the last will be the first,' or that in this life a Messiah will appear to bring forth into the light of the world which has cast them out the hidden honor of the pariah people. This simple state of affairs, and not the 'resentment' which is so strongly emphasized in Nietzsche's much admired construction in the *Genealogy of Morals*, is the source of the religiosity cultivated by pariah status groups. In passing, we may note that resentment may be accurately applied only to a limited extent; for one of Nietzsche's main examples, Buddhism, it is not at all applicable.

Incidentally, the development of status groups from ethnic segregations is by no means the normal phenomenon. On the contrary, since objective 'racial differences' are by no means basic to every subjective sentiment of an ethnic community, the ultimately racial foundation of status structure is rightly and absolutely a question of the concrete individual case. Very frequently a status group is instrumental in the production of a thoroughbred anthropological type. Certainly a status group is to a high degree effective in producing extreme types, for they select personally qualified individuals (e.g., the Knighthood selects those who are fit for warfare, physically and psychically). But selection is far from being the only, or the predominant, way in which status groups are formed: Political membership or class situation has at all times been at least as frequently decisive. And today the class situation is by far the predominant factor, for of course the possibility of a style of life expected for members of a status group is usually conditioned economically.

VIII. STATUS PRIVILEGES

For all practical purposes, stratification by status goes hand in hand with a monopolization of ideal and material goods or opportunities, in a manner we have come to know as typical. Besides the specific status honor, which always rests upon distance and exclusiveness, we find all sorts of material monopolies. Such honorific preferences may consist of the privilege of wearing special costumes, of eating special dishes taboo to others, of carrying arms—which is most obvious in its consequences—the right to pursue certain non-professional dilettante artistic practices, e.g., to play certain musical instruments. Of course, material monopolies provide the most effective motives for the exclusiveness of a status group; although, in themselves, they are rarely sufficient, almost always they come into play to some extent. Within a status circle there is the question of intermarriage: the interest of the families in the monopolization of potential bridegrooms is at least of equal importance and is parallel to the interest in the monopolization of daughters. The daughters of the circle must be provided for. With an increased inclosure of the status group, the conventional preferential opportunities for special employment grow into a legal monopoly of special offices for the members. Certain goods become objects for monopolization by status groups. In the typical fashion these include 'entailed estates' and frequently also the possessions of serfs or bondsmen and, finally, special trades. This monopolization occurs positively when the status group is exclusively entitled to own and to manage them; and negatively when, in order to maintain its specific way of life, the status group must *not* own and manage them.

The decisive role of a 'style of life' in status 'honor' means that status groups are the specific bearers of all 'conventions.' In whatever way it may be manifest, all 'stylization' of life either originates in status groups or is at least conserved by them. Even if the principles of status conventions differ greatly, they reveal certain typical traits, especially among those strata which are most privileged. Quite generally, among privileged status groups there is a status disqualification that operates against the performance of common physical labor. This disqualification is now 'setting in' in America against the old tradition of esteem for labor. Very frequently every rational economic pursuit, and especially 'entrepreneurial activity,' is looked upon as a disqualification of status. Artistic and literary activity is also considered as degrading work as soon as it is exploited for income, or at least when it is connected with hard physical exertion. An example is the sculptor working like a mason in his dusty smock as over against the painter in his salon-like 'studio' and those forms of musical practice that are acceptable to the status group.

IX. ECONOMIC CONDITIONS AND EFFECTS OF STATUS STRATIFICATION

The frequent disqualification of the gainfully employed as such is a direct result of the principle of status stratification peculiar to the social order, and of course, of this principle's opposition to a distribution of power which is regulated exclusively through the market. These two factors operate along with various individual ones, which will be touched upon below.

We have seen above that the market and its processes 'knows no personal distinctions': 'functional' interests dominate it. It knows nothing of 'honor.' The status order means precisely the reverse, viz.: stratification in terms of 'honor' and of styles of life peculiar to status groups as such. If mere economic acquisition and naked economic power still bearing the stigma of its extra-status origin could bestow upon anyone who has won it the same honor as those who are interested in status by virtue of style of life claim for themselves, the status order would be threatened at its very root. This is the more so as, given equality of status honor, property per se represents an addition even if it is not overtly acknowledged to be such. Yet if such economic acquisition and power gave the agent any honor at all, his wealth would result in his attaining more honor than those who successfully claim honor by virtue of style of life. Therefore all groups having interests in the status order react with special sharpness precisely against the pretensions of purely economic acquisition. In most cases they react the more vigorously the more they feel themselves threatened. Calderon's respectful treatment of the peasant, for instance, as opposed to Shakespeare's simultaneous and ostensible disdain of the canaille illustrates the different way in which a firmly structured status order reacts as compared with a status order that has become economically precarious. This is an example of a state of affairs that recurs everywhere. Precisely because of the rigorous reactions against the claims of property per se, the 'parvenu' is never accepted, personally and without reservation, by the privileged status groups, no matter how completely his style of life has been adjusted to theirs. They will only accept his descendants who have been educated in the conventions of their status group and who have never besmirched its honor by their own economic labor.

As to the general effect of the status order, only one consequence can be stated, but it is a very important one: the hindrance of the free development of the market occurs first for those goods which status groups directly withheld from free exchange by monopolization. This monopolization may be effected either legally or conventionally. For example, in many Hellenic cities during the epoch of status groups, and also originally in Rome, the inherited estate (as is shown by the old formula for indiction against spendthrifts) was monopolized just as were the estates of knights, peasants, priests, and especially the clientele of the craft and merchant guilds. The market is restricted, and the power of naked property per se, which gives its stamp to 'class formation,' is pushed into the background. The results of this process can be most varied. Of course, they do not necessarily weaken the contrasts in the economic situation. Frequently they strengthen these contrasts, and in any case, where stratification by status permeates a community as strongly as was the case in all political communities of antiquity and of the Middle Ages, one can never speak of a genuinely free market competition as we understand it today. There are wider effects than this direct exclusion of special goods from the market. From the contrariety between the status order and the purely economic order mentioned above, it follows that in most instances the notion of honor peculiar to status absolutely abhors that which is essential to the market: higgling. Honor abhors higgling among peers and occasionally it taboos higgling for the members of a status group in general. Therefore, everywhere some status groups, and usually the most influential, consider almost any kind of overt participation in economic acquisition as absolutely stigmatizing.

With some over-simplification, one might thus say that 'classes' are stratified according to their relations to the production and acquisition of goods; whereas 'status groups' are stratified according to the principles of their *consumption* of goods as represented by special 'styles of life.'

An 'occupational group' is also a status group. For normally, it successfully claims social honor only by virtue of the special style of life which may be determined by it. The differences between classes and status groups frequently overlap. It is precisely those status communities most strictly segregated in terms of honor (viz. the Indian castes) who today show, although within very rigid limits, a relatively high degree of indifference to pecuniary income. However, the Brahmins seek such income in many different ways.

As to the general economic conditions making for the predominance of stratification by 'status,' only very little can be said. When the bases of the acquisition and distribution of goods are relatively stable, stratification by status is favored. Every technological repercussion and economic transformation threatens stratification by status and pushes the class situation into the foreground. Epochs and countries in which the naked class situation is of predominant significance are regularly the periods of technical and economic transformations. And every slowing down of the shifting of economic stratifications leads, in due course, to the growth of status structures and makes for a resuscitation of the important role of social honor.

X. PARTIES

Whereas the genuine place of 'classes' is within the economic order, the place of 'status groups' is within the social order, that is, within the sphere of the distribution of 'honor.' From within these spheres, classes and status groups influence one another and they influence the legal order and are in turn influenced by it. But 'parties' live in a house of 'power.'

Their action is oriented toward the acquisition of social 'power,' that is to say, toward influencing a communal action no matter what its content may be. In principle, parties may exist in a social 'club' as well as in a 'state.' As over against the actions of classes and status groups, for which this is not necessarily the case, the communal actions of 'parties' always mean a societalization. For party actions are always directed toward a goal which is striven for in planned manner. This goal may be a 'cause' (the party may aim at realizing a program for ideal or material purposes), or the goal may be 'personal' (sinecures, power, and from these, honor for the leader and the followers of the party). Usually the party action aims at all these simultaneously. Parties are, therefore, only possible within communities that are societalized, that is, which have some rational order and a staff of persons available who are ready to enforce it. For parties aim precisely at influencing this staff, and if possible, to recruit it from party followers.

In any individual case, parties may represent interests determined through 'class situation' or 'status situation,' and they may recruit their following respectively from one or the other. But they need be neither purely 'class' nor purely 'status' parties. In most cases they are partly class parties and partly status parties, but sometimes they are neither. They may represent ephemeral or enduring structures. Their means of attaining power may be quite varied, ranging from naked violence of any sort to canvassing for votes with coarse or subtle means: money, social influence, the force of speech, suggestion, clumsy hoax, and so on to the rougher or more artful tactics of obstruction in parliamentary bodies.

The sociological structure of parties differs in a basic way according to the kind of communal action which they struggle to influence. Parties also differ according to whether or not the community is stratified by status or by classes. Above all else, they vary according to the structure of domination within the community. For their leaders normally deal with the conquest of a community. They are, in the general concept which is maintained here, not only products of specially modern forms of domination. We shall also designate as parties the ancient and medieval 'parties,' despite the fact that their structure differs basically from the structure of modern parties. By virtue of these structural differences of domination it is impossible to say anything about the structure of parties without discussing the structural forms of social domination per se. Parties, which are always structures struggling for domination, are very frequently organized in a very strict 'authoritarian' fashion. . .

Concerning 'classes,' 'status groups,' and 'parties,' it must be said in general that they necessarily presuppose a comprehensive societalization, and especially a political framework of communal action, within which they operate. This does not mean that parties would be confined by the frontiers of any individual political community. On the contrary, at all times it has been the order of the day that the societalization (even when it aims at the use of military force in common) reaches beyond the frontiers of politics. This has been the case in the solidarity of interests among the Oligarchs and among the democrats in Hellas, among the Guelfs and among Ghibellines in the Middle Ages, and within the Calvinist party during the period of religious struggles. It has been the case up to the solidarity of the landlords (international congress of agrarian landlords), and has continued among princes (holy alliance, Karlsbad de crees), socialist workers, conservatives (the longing of Prussian conservatives for Russian intervention in 1850). But their aim is not necessarily the establishment of new international political, i.e. *territorial*, dominion. In the main they aim to influence the existing dominion.[1]

[1] The posthumously published text breaks off here. We omit an incomplete sketch of types of 'warrior estates.'

6

Power and Bureaucracy*

I. THE BASIS OF LEGITIMACY

The definition, conditions, and types of imperative control. Imperative co-ordination' . . . [is] as the probability that certain specific commands (or all commands) from a given source will be obeyed by a given group of persons. It thus does not include every mode of exercising 'power' or 'influence' over other persons. The motives of obedience to commands in this sense can rest on considerations varying over a wide range from case to case; all the way from simple habituation to the most purely rational calculation of advantage. A criterion of every true relation of imperative control, however, is a certain minimum of voluntary submission; thus an interest (based on ulterior motives or genuine acceptance) in obedience.

Not every case of imperative co-ordination makes use of economic means; still less does it always have economic objectives. But normally (not always) the imperative co-ordination of the action of a considerable number of men requires control of a staff of persons. It is necessary, that is, that there should be a relatively high probability that the action of a definite, supposedly reliable group of persons will be primarily oriented to the execution of the supreme authority's general policy and specific commands.

The members of the administrative staff may be bound to obedience to their superior (or superiors) by custom, by affectual ties, by a purely material complex of interests, or by ideal (wertrational)

* The first part of this chapter is from The Theory of Social and Economic Organization, ed. Talcott Parsons (New York: The Free Press of Glencoe, Inc., 1947), pp. 324–45. Reprinted by permission of The Free Press and William Hodge & Company Limited. The entire chapter is from Wirtschaft und Gesellschaft.

motives. *Purely* material interests and calculations of advantage as the basis of solidarity between the chief and his administrative staff result, in this as in other connections, in a relatively unstable situation. Normally other elements, affectual and ideal, supplement such interests. In certain exceptional, temporary cases the former may be alone decisive. In everyday routine life these relationships, like others, are governed by custom and in addition, material calculation of advantage. But these factors, custom and personal advantage, purely affectual or ideal motives of solidarity, do not, even taken together, form a sufficiently reliable basis for a system of imperative co-ordination. In addition there is normally a further element, the belief in legitimacy.

It is an induction from experience that no system of authority voluntarily limits itself to the appeal to material or affectual or ideal motives as a basis for guaranteeing its continuance. In addition every such system attempts to establish and to cultivate the belief in its 'legitimacy.' But according to the kind of legitimacy which is claimed, the type of obedience, the kind of administrative staff developed to guarantee it, and the mode of exercising authority, will all differ fundamentally. Equally fundamental is the variation in effect. Hence, it is useful to classify the types of authority according to the kind of claim to legitimacy typically made by each. In doing this it is best to start from modern and therefore more familiar examples.

1. The choice of this rather than some other basis of classification can only be justified by its results. The fact that certain other typical criteria of variation are thereby neglected for the time being and can only be introduced at a later stage is not a decisive difficulty. The 'legitimacy' of a system of authority has far more than a merely 'ideal' significance, if only because it has very definite relations to the legitimacy of property.

2. Not every 'claim' which is protected by custom or by law should be spoken of as involving a relation of authority. Otherwise the worker, in his claim for fulfilment of the wage contract, would be exercising 'authority' over his employer because his claim can, on occasion, be enforced by order of a court. Actually his formal status is that of party to a contractual relationship with his employer, in which he has certain 'rights' to receive payments. At the same time the concept of a relation of authority naturally does not exclude the possibility that it has originated in a formally free contract. This is true of the authority of the employer over the worker as manifested

in the former's rules and instructions regarding the work process; and also of the authority of a feudal lord over a vassal who has freely entered into the relation of fealty. That subjection to military discipline is formally 'involuntary' while that to the discipline of the factory is voluntary does not alter the fact that the latter is also a case of subjection to authority. The position of a bureaucratic official is also entered into by contract and can be freely resigned, and even the status of 'subject' can often be freely entered into and (in certain circumstances) freely repudiated. Only in the limiting case of the slave is formal subjection to authority absolutely involuntary.

Another case, in some respects related, is that of economic 'power' based on monopolistic position; that is, in this case, the possibility of 'dictating' the terms of exchange to contractual partners. This will not, taken by itself, be considered to constitute 'authority' any more than any other kind of 'influence' which is derived from some kind of superiority, as by virtue of erotic attractiveness, skill in sport or in discussion. Even if a big bank is in a position to force other banks into a cartel arrangement, this will not alone be sufficient to justify calling it a relation of imperative co-ordination. But if there is an immediate relation of command and obedience such that the management of the first bank can give orders to the others with the claim that they shall, and the probability that they will, be obeyed purely as such regardless of particular content, and if their carrying out is supervised, it is another matter. Naturally, here as everywhere the transitions are gradual; there are all sorts of intermediate steps between mere indebtedness and debt slavery. Even the position of a 'salon' can come very close to the borderline of authoritarian domination and yet not necessarily constitute a system of authority. Sharp differentiation in concrete fact is often impossible, but this makes clarity in the analytical distinctions all the more important.

3. Naturally, the legitimacy of a system of authority may be treated sociologically only as the probability that to a relevant degree the appropriate attitudes will exist, and the corresponding practical conduct ensue. It is by no means true that every case of submissiveness to persons in positions of power is primarily (or even at all) oriented to this belief. Loyalty may be hypocritically simulated by individuals or by whole groups on purely opportunistic grounds, or carried out in practice for reasons of material self-interest. Or people may submit from individual weakness and helplessness because there is no acceptable alternative. But these considerations are not decisive for the clas-

cification of types of imperative co-ordination. What is important is the fact that in a given case the particular claim to legitimacy is to a significant degree and according to its type treated as 'valid'; that this fact confirms the position of the persons claiming authority and that it helps to determine the choice of means of its exercise.

Furthermore a system of imperative co-ordination may—as often occurs in practice—be so completely assured of dominance, on the one hand by the obvious community of interests between the chief and his administrative staff as opposed to the subjects (bodyguards, Pretorians, 'red' or 'white' guards), on the other hand by the helplessness of the latter, that it can afford to drop even the pretence of a claim to legitimacy. But even then the mode of legitimation of the relation between chief and his staff may vary widely according to the type of basis of the relation of authority between them, and, as will be shown, this variation is highly significant for the structure of imperative co-ordination.

4. 'Obedience' will be taken to mean that the action of the person obeying follows in essentials such a course that the content of the command may be taken to have become the basis of action for its own sake. Furthermore, the fact that it is so taken is referable only to the formal obligation, without regard to the actor's own attitude to the value or lack of value of the content of the command as such.

5. Subjectively, the causal sequence may vary, especially as between 'submission' and 'sympathetic agreement.' This distinction is not, however, significant for the present classification of types of authority.

6. The scope of determination of social relationships and cultural phenomena by authority and imperative co-ordination is considerably broader than appears at first sight. For instance, the authority exercised in the school has much to do with the determination of the forms of speech and of written language which are regarded as orthodox. The official languages of autonomous political units, hence of their ruling groups, have often become in this sense orthodox forms of speech and writing and have even led to the formation of separate 'nations' (for instance, the separation of Holland from Germany). The authority of parents and of the school, however, extends far beyond the determination of such cultural patterns which are perhaps only apparently formal, to the formation of the character of the young, and hence of human beings generally.

7. The fact that the chief and his administrative staff often appear formally as servants or agents of those they rule, naturally does noth-

ing whatever to disprove the authoritarian character of the relationship. There will be occasion later to speak of the substantive features of so-called 'democracy.' But a certain minimum of assured power to issue commands, thus of 'authority,' must be provided for in nearly every conceivable case.

The three pure types of legitimate authority. There are three pure types of legitimate authority. The validity of their claims to legitimacy may be based on:

1. Rational grounds—resting on a belief in the 'legality' of patterns of normative rules and the right of those elevated to authority under such rules to issue commands (legal authority).

2. Traditional grounds—resting on an established belief in the sanctity of immemorial traditions and the legitimacy of the status of those exercising authority under them (traditional authority); or finally,

3. Charismatic grounds—resting on devotion to the specific and exceptional sanctity, heroism or exemplary character of an individual person, and of the normative patterns or order revealed or ordained by him (charismatic authority).

In the case of legal authority, obedience is owed to the legally established impersonal order. It extends to the persons exercising the authority of office under it only by virtue of the formal legality of their commands and only within the scope of authority of the office. In the case of traditional authority, obedience is owed to the *person* of the chief who occupies the traditionally sanctioned position of authority and who is (within its sphere) bound by tradition. But here the obligation of obedience is not based on the impersonal order, but is a matter of personal loyalty within the area of accustomed obligations. In the case of charismatic authority, it is the charismatically qualified leader as such who is obeyed by virtue of personal trust in him and his revelation, his heroism or his exemplary qualities so far as they fall within the scope of the individual's belief in his charisma.

1. The usefulness of the above classification can only be judged by its results in promoting systematic analysis. The concept of 'charisma' ('the gift of grace') is taken from the vocabulary of early Christianity. For the Christian religious organization Rudolf Sohm, in his *Kirchenrecht*, was the first to clarify the substance of the concept, even though he did not use the same terminology. Others (for instance, Hollin, *Enthusiasmus und Bussgewalt*) have clarified certain important consequences of it. It is thus nothing new.

2. The fact that none of these three ideal types, the elucidation of

which will occupy the following pages, is usually to be found in historical cases in 'pure' form, is naturally not a valid objection to attempting their conceptual formulation in the sharpest possible form. In this respect the present case is no different from many others. Later on the transformation of pure charisma by the process of routinization will be discussed and thereby the relevance of the concept to the understanding of empirical systems of authority considerably increased. But even so it may be said of every empirically historical phenomenon of authority that it is not likely to be 'as an open book.' Analysis in terms of sociological types has, after all, as compared with purely empirical historical investigation, certain advantages which should not be minimized. That is, it can in the particular case of a concrete form of authority determine what conforms to or approximates such types as 'charisma,' 'hereditary charisma,' 'the charisma of office,' 'patriarchy,' 'bureaucracy,' the authority of status groups,[1] and in doing so it can work with relatively unambiguous concepts. But the idea that the whole of concrete historical reality can be exhausted in the conceptual scheme about to be developed is as far from the author's thoughts as anything could be.

II. LEGAL AUTHORITY WITH A BUREAUCRATIC ADMINISTRATIVE STAFF[2]

Legal authority: the pure type with employment of a bureaucratic administrative staff. The effectiveness of legal authority rests on the acceptance of the validity of the following mutually interdependent ideas.

1. That any given legal norm may be established by agreement or by imposition, on grounds of expediency or rational values or both, with a claim to obedience at least on the part of the members of the corporate group. This is, however, usually extended to include all persons within the sphere of authority or of power in question—which in the case of territorial bodies is the territorial area—who stand in certain social relationships or carry out forms of social action

[1] *Ständische.* There is no really acceptable English rendering of this term.—ED. [Parsons' footnote]
[2] The specifically modern type of administration has intentionally been taken as a point of departure in order to make it possible later to contrast the others with it.

which in the order governing the corporate group have been declared to be relevant.

2. That every body of law consists essentially in a consistent system of abstract rules which have normally been intentionally established. Furthermore, administration of law is held to consist in the application of these rules to particular cases; the administrative process in the rational pursuit of the interests which are specified in the order governing the corporate group within the limits laid down by legal precepts and following principles which are capable of generalized formulation and are approved in the order governing the group, or at least not disapproved in it.

3. That thus the typical person in authority occupies an 'office.' In the action associated with his status, including the commands he issues to others, he is subject to an impersonal order to which his actions are oriented. This is true not only for persons exercising legal authority who are in the usual sense 'officials,' but, for instance, for the elected president of a state.

4. That the person who obeys authority does so, as it is usually stated, only in his capacity as a 'member' of the corporate group and what he obeys is only 'the law.' He may in this connection be the member of an association, of a territorial commune, of a church, or a citizen of a state.

5. In conformity with point 3, it is held that the members of the corporate group, in so far as they obey a person in authority, do not owe this obedience to him as an individual, but to the impersonal order. Hence, it follows that there is an obligation to obedience only within the sphere of the rationally delimited authority which, in terms of the order, has been conferred upon him.

The following may thus be said to be the fundamental categories of rational legal authority:—

(1) A continuous organization of official functions bound by rules.

(2) A specified sphere of competence. This involves (a) a sphere of obligations to perform functions which has been marked off as part of a systematic division of labour. (b) The provision of the incumbent with the necessary authority to carry out these functions. (c) That the necessary means of compulsion are clearly defined and their use is subject to definite conditions. A unit exercising authority which is organized in this way will be called an 'administrative organ.' (Behörde)

There are administrative organs in this sense in large-scale private organizations, in parties and armies, as well as in the state and the church. An elected president, a cabinet of ministers, or a body of elected representatives also in this sense constitute administrative organs. This is not, however, the place to discuss these concepts. Not every administrative organ is provided with compulsory powers. But this distinction is not important for present purposes.

(3) The organization of offices follows the principle of hierarchy; that is, each lower office is under the control and supervision of a higher one. There is a right of appeal and of statement of grievances from the lower to the higher. Hierarchies differ in respect to whether and in what cases complaints can lead to a ruling from an authority at various points higher in the scale, and as to whether changes are imposed from higher up or the responsibility for such changes is left to the lower office, the conduct of which was the subject of complaint.

(4) The rules which regulate the conduct of an office may be technical rules or norms.[3] In both cases, if their application is to be fully rational, specialized training is necessary. It is thus normally true that only a person who has demonstrated an adequate technical training is qualified to be a member of the administrative staff of such an organized group, and hence only such persons are eligible for appointment to official positions. The administrative staff of a rational corporate group thus typically consists of 'officials,' whether the organization be devoted to political, religious, economic—in particular, capitalistic—or other ends.

(5) In the rational type it is a matter of principle that the members of the administrative staff should be completely separated from ownership of the means of production or administration. Officials, employees, and workers attached to the administrative staff do not themselves own the non-human means of production and administration. These are rather provided for their use in kind or in money, and the official is obligated to render an accounting of their use. There exists, furthermore, in principle complete separation of the property belonging to the organization, which is controlled within the sphere

[3] Weber does not explain this distinction. By a 'technical rule' he probably means a prescribed course of action which is dictated primarily on grounds touching efficiency of the performance of the immediate functions, while by 'norms' he probably means rules which limit conduct on grounds other than those of efficiency. Of course, in one sense all rules are norms in that they are prescriptions for conduct, conformity with which is problematical.—ED. [Parsons' footnote]

of office, and the personal property of the official, which is available for his own private uses. There is a corresponding separation of the place in which official functions are carried out, the 'office' in the sense of premises, from living quarters.

(6) In the rational type case, there is also a complete absence of appropriation of his official position by the incumbent. Where 'rights' to an office exist, as in the case of judges, and recently of an increasing proportion of officials and even of workers, they do not normally serve the purpose of appropriation by the official, but of securing the purely objective and independent character of the conduct of the office so that it is oriented only to the relevant norms.

(7) Administrative acts, decisions, and rules are formulated and recorded in writing, even in cases where oral discussion is the rule or is even mandatory. This applies at least to preliminary discussions and proposals, to final decisions, and to all sorts of orders and rules. The combination of written documents and a continuous organization of official functions constitutes the 'office' [4] which is the central focus of all types of modern corporate action.

(8) Legal authority can be exercised in a wide variety of different forms which will be distinguished and discussed later. The following analysis will be deliberately confined for the most part to the aspect cf imperative co-ordination in the structure of the administrative staff. It will consist in an analysis in terms of ideal types of officialdom or 'bureaucracy.'

In the above outline no mention has been made of the kind of supreme head appropriate to a system of legal authority. This is a consequence of certain considerations which can only be made entirely understandable at a later stage in the analysis. There are very important types of rational imperative co-ordination which, with respect to the ultimate source of authority, belong to other categories.

[4] *Bureau*. It has seemed necessary to use the English word 'office' in three different meanings, which are distinguished in Weber's discussion by at least two terms. The first is *Amt*, which means 'office' in the sense of the institutionally defined status of a person. The second is the 'work premises' as in the expression 'he spent the afternoon in his office.' For this Weber uses *Bureau* as also for the third meaning which he has just defined, the 'organized work process of a group.' In this last sense an office is a particular type of 'organization,' or *Betrieb* in Weber's sense. This use is established in English in such expressions as 'the District Attorney's Office has such and such functions.' Which of the three meanings is involved in a given case will generally be clear from the context.—ED. [Parsons' footnote]

This is true of the hereditary charismatic type, as illustrated by hereditary monarchy and of the pure charismatic type of a president chosen by plebiscite. Other cases involve rational elements at important points, but are made up of a combination of bureaucratic and charismatic components, as is true of the cabinet form of government. Still others are subject to the authority of the chief of other corporate groups, whether their character be charismatic or bureaucratic; thus the formal head of a government department under a parliamentary regime may be a minister who occupies his position because of his authority in a party. The type of rational, legal administrative staff is capable of application in all kinds of situations and contexts. It is the most important mechanism for the administration of everyday profane affairs. For in that sphere, the exercise of authority and, more broadly, imperative co-ordination, consists precisely in administration.

The purest type of exercise of legal authority is that which employs a bureaucratic administrative staff. Only the supreme chief of the organization occupies his position of authority by virtue of appropriation, of election, or of having been designated for the succession. But even *his* authority consists in a sphere of legal 'competence.' The whole administrative staff under the supreme authority then consists, in the purest type, of individual officials who are appointed and function according to the following criteria:

(1) They are personally free and subject to authority only with respect to their impersonal official obligations.

(2) They are organized in a clearly defined hierarchy of offices.

(3) Each office has a clearly defined sphere of competence in the legal sense.

(4) The office is filled by a free contractual relationship. Thus, in principle, there is free selection.

(5) Candidates are selected on the basis of technical qualifications. In the most rational case, this is tested by examination or guaranteed by diplomas certifying technical training, or both. They are *appointed*, not elected.

(6) They are remunerated by fixed salaries in money, for the most part with a right to pensions. Only under certain circumstances does the employing authority, especially in private organizations, have a right to terminate the appointment, but the official is always free to resign. The salary scale is primarily graded according to rank in the hierarchy; but in addition to this criterion, the responsibility of the

position and the requirements of the incumbent's social status may be taken into account.

(7) The office is treated as the sole, or at least the primary, occupation of the incumbent.

(8) It constitutes a career. There is a system of 'promotion' according to seniority or to achievement, or both. Promotion is dependent on the judgment of superiors.

(9) The official works entirely separated from ownership of the means of administration and without appropriation of his position.

(10) He is subject to strict and systematic discipline and control in the conduct of the office.

This type of organization is in principle applicable with equal facility to a wide variety of different fields. It may be applied in profit-making business or in charitable organizations, or in any number of other types of private enterprises serving ideal or material ends. It is equally applicable to political and to religious organizations. With varying degrees of approximation to a pure type, its historical existence can be demonstrated in all these fields.

1. For example, this type of bureaucracy is found in private clinics, as well as in endowed hospitals or the hospitals maintained by religious orders. Bureaucratic organization has played a major role in the Catholic Church. It is well illustrated by the administrative role of the priesthood (*Kaplanokratie*) in the modern church, which has expropriated almost all of the old church benefices, which were in former days to a large extent subject to private appropriation. It is also illustrated by the conception of the universal Episcopate, which is thought of as formally constituting a universal legal competence in religious matters. Similarly, the doctrine of Papal infallibility is thought of as in fact involving a universal competence, but only one which functions 'ex cathedra' in the sphere of the office, thus implying the typical distinction between the sphere of office and that of the private affairs of the incumbent. The same phenomena are found in the large-scale capitalistic enterprise; and the larger it is, the greater their role. And this is not less true of political parties, which will be discussed separately. Finally, the modern army is essentially a bureaucratic organization administered by that peculiar type of military functionary, the 'officer.'

2. Bureaucratic authority is carried out in its purest form where it is most clearly dominated by the principle of appointment. There is no such thing as a hierarchy of elected officials in the same sense as

there is a hierarchical organization of appointed officials. In the first place, election makes it impossible to attain a stringency of discipline even approaching that in the appointed type. For it is open to a subordinate official to compete for elective honours on the same terms as his superiors, and his prospects are not dependent on the superior's judgment.

3. Appointment by free contract, which makes free selection possible, is essential to modern bureaucracy. Where there is a hierarchical organization with impersonal spheres of competence, but occupied by unfree officials—like slaves or dependents, who, however, function in a formally bureaucratic manner—the term 'patrimonial bureaucracy' will be used.

4. The role of technical qualifications in bureaucratic organizations is continually increasing. Even an official in a party or a trade-union organization is in need of specialized knowledge, though it is usually of an empirical character, developed by experience, rather than by formal training. In the modern state, the only 'offices' for which no technical qualifications are required are those of ministers and presidents. This only goes to prove that they are 'officials' only in a formal sense, and not substantively, as is true of the managing director or president of a large business corporation. There is no question but that the 'position' of the capitalistic entrepreneur is as definitely appropriated as is that of a monarch. Thus at the top of a bureaucratic organization, there is necessarily an element which is at least not purely bureaucratic. The category of bureaucracy is one applying only to the exercise of control by means of a particular kind of administrative staff.

5. The bureaucratic official normally receives a fixed salary. By contrast, sources of income which are privately appropriated will be called 'benefices.' Bureaucratic salaries are also normally paid in money. Though this is not essential to the concept of bureaucracy, it is the arrangement which best fits the pure type. Payments in kind are apt to have the character of benefices, and the receipt of a benefice normally implies the appropriation of opportunities for earnings and of positions. . . .

*Technical advantages of bureaucratic organization.** The decisive

---

* This second part of the chapter is from *From Max Weber: Essays in Sociology,* ed. and trans. Hans Gerth and C. Wright Mills (New York: Oxford University Press, Inc., 1946), pp. 214–16, 228–30. Copyright 1946 by Oxford University Press, Inc. Reprinted by permission.

reason for the advance of bureaucratic organization has always been its purely technical superiority over any other form of organization. The fully developed bureaucratic mechanism compares with other organizations exactly as does the machine with the non-mechanical modes of production.

Precision, speed, unambiguity, knowledge of the files, continuity, discretion, unity, strict subordination, reduction of friction and of material and personal costs—these are raised to the optimum point in the strictly bureaucratic administration, and especially in its monocratic form. As compared with all collegiate, honorific, and avocational forms of administration, trained bureaucracy is superior on all these points. And as far as complicated tasks are concerned, paid bureaucratic work is not only more precise but, in the last analysis, it is often cheaper than even formally unremunerated honorific service.

Honorific arrangements make administrative work an avocation and, for this reason alone, honorific service normally functions more slowly; being less bound to schemata and being more formless. Hence it is less precise and less unified than bureaucratic work because it is less dependent upon superiors and because the establishment and exploitation of the apparatus of subordinate officials and filing services are almost unavoidably less economical. Honorific service is less continuous than bureaucratic and frequently quite expensive. This is especially the case if one thinks not only of the money costs to the public treasury—costs which bureaucratic administration, in comparison with administration by notables, usually substantially increases—but also of the frequent economic losses of the governed caused by delays and lack of precision. The possibility of administration by notables normally and permanently exists only where official management can be satisfactorily discharged as an avocation. With the qualitative increase of tasks the administration has to face, administration by notables reaches its limits—today, even in England. Work organized by collegiate bodies causes friction and delay and requires compromises between colliding interests and views. The administration, therefore, runs less precisely and is more independent of superiors; hence, it is less unified and slower. All advances of the Prussian administrative organization have been and will in the future be advances of the bureaucratic, and especially of the monocratic, principle.

Today, it is primarily the capitalist market economy which demands that the official business of the administration be discharged precisely, unambiguously, continuously, and with as much speed as possible. Normally, the very large, modern capitalist enterprises are themselves unequalled models of strict bureaucratic organization. Business management throughout rests on increasing precision, steadiness, and, above all, the speed of operations. This, in turn, is determined by the peculiar nature of the modern means of communication, including, among other things, the news service of the press. The extraordinary increase in the speed by which public announcements, as well as economic and political facts, are transmitted exerts a steady and sharp pressure in the direction of speeding up the tempo of administrative reaction towards various situations. The optimum of such reaction time is normally attained only by a strictly bureaucratic organization.[5]

Bureaucratization offers above all the optimum possibility for carrying through the principle of specializing administrative functions according to purely objective considerations. Individual performances are allocated to functionaries who have specialized training and who by constant practice learn more and more. The 'objective' discharge of business primarily means a discharge of business according to *calculable rules* and 'without regard for persons.'

'Without regard for persons' is also the watchword of the 'market' and, in general, of all pursuits of naked economic interests. A consistent execution of bureaucratic domination means the leveling of status 'honor.' Hence, if the principle of the free-market is not at the same time restricted, it means the universal domination of the 'class situation.' That this consequence of bureaucratic domination has not set in everywhere, parallel to the extent of bureaucratization, is due to the differences among possible principles by which polities may meet their demands.

The second element mentioned, 'calculable rules,' also is of paramount importance for modern bureaucracy. The peculiarity of modern culture, and specifically of its technical and economic basis, demands this very 'calculability' of results. When fully developed, bureaucracy also stands, in a specific sense, under the principle of *sine ira ac studio*. Its specific nature, which is welcomed by capitalism, develops the more perfectly the more the bureaucracy is 'dehumanized,' the more completely it succeeds in eliminating from official

---

[5] Here we cannot discuss in detail how the bureaucratic apparatus may, and actually does, produce definite obstacles to the discharge of business in a manner suitable for the single case.

business love, hatred, and all purely personal, irrational, and emotional elements which escape calculation. This is the specific nature of bureaucracy and it is appraised as its special virtue.

The more complicated and specialized modern culture becomes, the more its external supporting apparatus demands the personally detached and strictly 'objective' expert, in lieu of the master of older social structures, who was moved by personal sympathy and favor, by grace and gratitude. Bureaucracy offers the attitudes demanded by the external apparatus of modern culture in the most favorable combination. As a rule, only bureaucracy has established the foundation for the administration of a rational law conceptually systematized on the basis of such enactments as the latter Roman imperial period first created with a high degree of technical perfection. During the Middle Ages, this law was received along with the bureaucratization of legal administration, that is to say, with the displacement of the old trial procedure which was bound to tradition or to irrational presuppositions, by the rationally trained and specialized expert.

.　.　.　.　.　.

The permanent character of the bureaucratic machine. Once it is fully established, bureaucracy is among those social structures which are the hardest to destroy. Bureaucracy is the means of carrying 'community action' over into rationally ordered 'societal action.' Therefore, as an instrument for 'societalizing' relations of power, bureaucracy has been and is a power instrument of the first order—for the one who controls the bureaucratic apparatus.

Under otherwise equal conditions, a 'societal action,' which is methodically ordered and led, is superior to every resistance of 'mass' or even of 'communal action.' And where the bureaucratization of administration has been completely carried through, a form of power relation is established that is practically unshatterable.

The individual bureaucrat cannot squirm out of the apparatus in which he is harnessed. In contrast to the honorific or avocational 'notable,' the professional bureaucrat is chained to his activity by his entire material and ideal existence. In the great majority of cases, he is only a single cog in an ever-moving mechanism which prescribes to him an essentially fixed route of march. The official is entrusted with specialized tasks and normally the mechanism cannot be put into motion or arrested by him, but only from the very top. The individual bureaucrat is thus forged to the community of all the functionaries who are integrated into the mechanism. They have a common interest in seeing that the mechanism continues its functions and that the societally exercised authority carries on.

The ruled, for their part, cannot dispense with or replace the bureaucratic apparatus of authority once it exists. For this bureaucracy rests upon expert training, a functional specialization of work, and an attitude set for habitual and virtuoso-like mastery of single yet methodically integrated functions. If the official stops working, or if his work is forcefully interrupted, chaos results, and it is difficult to improvise replacements from among the governed who are fit to master such chaos. This holds for public administration as well as for private economic management. More and more the material fate of the masses depends upon the steady and correct functioning of the increasingly bureaucratic organizations of private capitalism. The idea of eliminating these organizations becomes more and more utopian.

The discipline of officialdom refers to the attitude-set of the official for precise obedience within his *habitual* activity, in public as well as in private organizations. This discipline increasingly becomes the basis of all order, however great the practical importance of administration on the basis of the filed documents may be. The naive idea of Bakuninism of destroying the basis of 'acquired rights' and 'domination' by destroying public documents overlooks the settled orientation of man for keeping to the habitual rules and regulations that continue to exist independently of the documents. Every reorganization of beaten or dissolved troops, as well as the restoration of administrative orders destroyed by revolt, panic, or other catastrophes, is realized by appealing to the trained orientation of obedient compliance to such orders. Such compliance has been conditioned into the officials, on the one hand, and, on the other hand, into the governed. If such an appeal is successful it brings, as it were, the disturbed mechanism into gear again.

The objective indispensability of the once-existing apparatus, with its peculiar, 'impersonal' character, means that the mechanism—in contrast to feudal orders based upon personal piety—is easily made to work for anybody who knows how to gain control over it. A rationally ordered system of officials continues to function smoothly after the enemy has occupied the area; he merely needs to change the top officials. This body of officials continues to operate because it is to the vital interest of everyone concerned, including above all the enemy.

During the course of his long years in power, Bismarck brought his ministerial colleagues into unconditional bureaucratic dependence by eliminating all independent statesmen. Upon his retirement, he saw to his surprise that they continued to manage their offices unconcerned and undismayed, as if he had not been the master mind and creator of these creatures, but rather as if some single figure had been exchanged for some other figure in the bureaucratic machine. With all the changes of masters in France since the time of the First Empire, the power machine has remained essentially the same. Such a machine makes 'revolution,' in the sense of the forceful creation of entirely new formations of authority, technically more and more impossible, especially when the apparatus controls the modern means of communication (telegraph, et cetera) and also by virtue of its internal rationalized structure. In classic fashion, France has demonstrated how this process has substituted *coups d'état* for 'revolutions': all successful transformations in France have amounted to *coups d'état.*

. . . . .

III. TRADITIONAL AUTHORITY*

Traditional authority. A system of imperative co-ordination will be called 'traditional' if legitimacy is claimed for it and believed in on the basis of the sanctity of the order and the attendant powers of control as they have been handed down from the past, 'have always existed.' The person or persons exercising authority are designated according to traditionally transmitted rules. The object of obedience is the personal authority of the individual which he enjoys by virtue of his traditional status. The organized group exercising authority is, in the simplest case, primarily based on relations of personal loyalty, cultivated through a common process of education. The person exercising authority is not a 'superior,' but a personal 'chief' (*Heer*).

His administrative staff does not consist primarily of officials, but of personal retainers. Those subject to authority are not 'members' of

---

* This final part of the chapter is from *The Theory of Social and Economic Organization,* ed. Talcott Parsons (New York: The Free Press of Glencoe, Inc., 1947), pp. 341–42, 358–63.

an association, but are either his traditional 'comrades' or his 'subjects.' What determines the relations of the administrative staff to the chief is not the impersonal obligation of office, but personal loyalty to the chief.

Obedience is not owed to enacted rules, but to the person who occupies a position of authority by tradition or who has been chosen for such a position on a traditional basis. His commands are legitimized in one of two ways: (a) partly in terms of traditions which themselves directly determine the content of the command and the objects and extent of authority. In so far as this is true, to overstep the traditional limitations would endanger his traditional status by undermining acceptance of his legitimacy. (b) In part, it is a matter of the chief's free personal decision, in that tradition leaves a certain sphere open for this. This sphere of traditional prerogative rests primarily on the fact that the obligations of obedience on the basis of personal loyalty are essentially unlimited.[6] There is thus a double sphere: on the one hand, of action which is bound to specific tradition; on the other hand, of that which is free of any specific rules.

In the latter sphere, the chief is free to confer 'grace' on the basis of his personal pleasure or displeasure, his personal likes and dislikes, quite arbitrarily, particularly in return for gifts which often become a source of regular income. So far as his action follows principles at all, these are principles of substantive ethical common sense, of justice, or of utilitarian expediency. They are not, however, as in the case of legal authority, formal principles. The exercise of authority is normally oriented to the question of what the chief and his administrative staff will normally permit, in view of the traditional obedience of the subjects and what will or will not arouse their resistance. When resistance occurs, it is directed against the person of the chief or of a member of his staff. The accusation is that he has failed to observe the traditional limits of his authority. Opposition is not directed against the system as such.

It is impossible in the pure type of traditional authority for law or administrative rules to be deliberately created by legislation. What

[6] This does not seem to be a very happy formulation of the essential point. It is not necessary that the authority of a person in such a position, such as the head of a household, should be unlimited. It is rather that its extent is unspecified. It is generally limited by higher obligations, but the burden of proof rests upon the person on whom an obligation is laid that there is such a conflicting higher obligation.—ED. [Parsons' footnote]

is actually new is thus claimed to have always been in force but only recently to have become known through the wisdom of the promulgator. The only documents which can play a part in the orientation of legal administration are the documents of tradition; namely, precedents.

. . . . .

IV. CHARISMATIC AUTHORITY

The principal characteristics of charismatic authority and its relation to forms of communal organization. The term 'charisma' will be applied to a certain quality of an individual personality by virtue of which he is set apart from ordinary men and treated as endowed with supernatural, superhuman, or at least specifically exceptional powers or qualities. These are such as are not accessible to the ordinary person, but are regarded as of divine origin or as exemplary, and on the basis of them the individual concerned is treated as a leader. In primitive circumstances this peculiar kind of deference is paid to prophets, to people with a reputation for therapeutic or legal wisdom, to leaders in the hunt, and heroes in war. It is very often thought of as resting on magical powers. How the quality in question would be ultimately judged from any ethical, aesthetic, or other such point of view is naturally entirely indifferent for purposes of definition. What is alone important is how the individual is actually regarded by those subject to charismatic authority, by his 'followers' or 'disciples.'

For present purposes it will be necessary to treat a variety of different types as being endowed with charisma in this sense. It includes the state of a 'berserker' whose spells of maniac passion have, apparently wrongly, sometimes been attributed to the use of drugs. In Medieval Byzantium a group of people endowed with this type of charismatic war-like passion were maintained as a kind of weapon. It includes the 'shaman,' the kind of magician who in the pure type is subject to epileptoid seizures as a means of falling into trances. Another type is that of Joseph Smith, the founder of Mormonism, who, however, cannot be classified in this way with absolute certainty since there is a possibility that he was a very sophisticated type of deliberate swindler. Finally it includes the type of intellectual, such as Kurt Eisner,[7] who is carried away with his own demagogic success. Sociological analysis, which must abstain from value judgments, will treat all these on the same level as the men who, according to conventional judgments, are the 'greatest' heroes, prophets, and saviours.

1. It is recognition on the part of those subject to authority which is decisive for the validity of charisma. This is freely given and guaranteed by what is held to be a 'sign' or proof, originally always a miracle, and consists in devotion to the corresponding revelation, hero worship, or absolute trust in the leader. But where charisma is genuine, it is not this which is the basis of the claim to legitimacy. This basis lies rather in the conception that it is the duty of those who have been called to a charismatic mission to recognize its quality and to act accordingly. Psychologically this 'recognition' is a matter of complete personal devotion to the possessor of the quality, arising out of enthusiasm, or of despair and hope.

No prophet has ever regarded his quality as dependent on the attitudes of the masses toward him. No elective king or military leader has ever treated those who have resisted him or tried to ignore him otherwise than as delinquent in duty. Failure to take part in a military expedition under such leader, even though recruitment is formally voluntary, has universally been met with disdain.

2. If proof of his charismatic qualification fails him for long, the leader endowed with charisma tends to think his god or his magical or heroic powers have deserted him. If he is for long unsuccessful, above all if his leadership fails to benefit his followers, it is likely that his charismatic authority will disappear. This is the genuine charismatic meaning of the 'gift of grace.'

Even the old Germanic kings were sometimes rejected with scorn. Similar phenomena are very common among so-called 'primitive' peoples. In China the charismatic quality of the monarch, which was transmitted unchanged by heredity, was upheld so rigidly that any misfortune whatever, not only defeats in war, but drought, floods, or astronomical phenomena which were considered unlucky, forced him to do public penance and might even force his abdication. If such things occurred, it was a sign that he did not possess the requisite charismatic virtue, he was thus not a legitimate 'Son of Heaven.'

3. The corporate group which is subject to charismatic authority is based on an emotional form of communal relationship. The ad-

[7] The leader of the communistic experiment in Bavaria in 1919.—ED. [Parsons' footnote]

ministrative staff of a charismatic leader does not consist of 'officials';
at least its members are not technically trained. It is not chosen on
the basis of social privilege nor from the point of view of domestic
or personal dependency. It is rather chosen in terms of the charismatic
qualities of its members. The prophet has his disciples; the war lord
his selected henchmen; the leader, generally, his followers. There is
no such thing as 'appointment' or 'dismissal,' no career, no promotion.
There is only a 'call' at the instance of the leader on the basis of the
charismatic qualification of those he summons. There is no hierarchy;
the leader merely intervenes in general or in individual cases when
he considers the members of his staff inadequate to a task with which
they have been entrusted. There is no such thing as a definite sphere
of authority and of competence, and no appropriation of official
powers on the basis of social privileges. There may, however, be territorial or functional limits to charismatic powers and to the individual's 'mission.' There is no such thing as a salary or a benefice. Disciples or followers tend to live primarily in a communistic relationship
with their leader on means which have been provided by voluntary
gift. There are no established administrative organs. In their place
are agents who have been provided with charismatic authority by
their chief or who possess charisma of their own. There is no system
of formal rules, of abstract legal principles, and hence no process of
judicial decision oriented to them. But equally there is no legal
wisdom oriented to judicial precedent. Formally concrete judgments
are newly created from case to case and are originally regarded as
divine judgments and revelations. From a substantive point of view,
every charismatic authority would have to subscribe to the proposi-
tion, 'It is written . . . , but I say unto you. . .' The genuine
prophet, like the genuine military leader and every true leader in this
sense, preaches, creates, or demands new obligations. In the pure type
of charisma, these are imposed on the authority of revolution by
oracles, or of the leader's own will, and are recognized by the members
of the religious, military, or party group, because they come from
such a source. Recognition is a duty. When such an authority comes
into conflict with the competing authority of another who also claims
charismatic sanction, the only recourse is to some kind of a contest,
by magical means or even an actual physical battle of the leaders. In
principle, only one side can be in the right in such a conflict; the
other must be guilty of a wrong which has to be expiated.

Charismatic authority is thus specifically outside the realm of every-

day routine and the profane sphere. In this respect, it is sharply opposed both to rational, and particularly bureaucratic, authority, and
to traditional authority, whether in its patriarchal, patrimonial, or any
other form. Both rational and traditional authority are specifically
forms of everyday routine control of action; while the charismatic
type is the direct antithesis of this. Bureaucratic authority is specifically rational in the sense of being bound to intellectually analysable
rules; while charismatic authority is specifically irrational in the sense
of being foreign to all rules. Traditional authority is bound to the
precedents handed down from the past and to this extent is also
oriented to rules. Within the sphere of its claims, charismatic authority repudiates the past, and is in this sense a specifically revolutionary
force. It recognizes no appropriation of positions of power by virtue
of the possession of property, either on the part of a chief or of socially
privileged groups. The only basis of legitimacy for it is personal
charisma, so long as it is proved; that is, as long as it receives recognition and is able to satisfy the followers or disciples. But this lasts only
so long as the belief in its charismatic inspiration remains.

The above is scarcely in need of further discussion. What has been
said applies to the position of authority of such elected monarchs as
Napoleon, with his use of the plebiscite. It applies to the 'rule of
genius,' which has elevated people of humble origin to thrones and
high military commands, just as much as it applies to religious
prophets or war heroes.

4. Pure charisma is specifically foreign to economic considerations.
Whenever it appears, it constitutes a 'call' in the most emphatic sense
of the word, a 'mission' or a 'spiritual duty.' In the pure type, it dis-
dains and repudiates economic exploitation of the gifts of grace as a
source of income, though, to be sure, this often remains more an ideal
than a fact. It is not that charisma always means the renunciation
of property or even of acquisition, as under certain circumstances
prophets and their disciples do. The heroic warrior and his followers
actively seek 'booty'; the elective ruler or the charismatic party leader
requires the material means of power. The former in addition requires
a brilliant display of his authority to bolster his prestige. What is
despised, so long as the genuinely charismatic type is adhered to, is
traditional or rational everyday economizing, the attainment of a
regular income by continuous economic activity devoted to this end.
Support by gifts, sometimes on a grand scale involving foundations,

even by bribery and grand-scale honoraria, or by begging, constitute
the strictly voluntary type of support. On the other hand, 'booty,' or
coercion, whether by force or by other means, is the other typical
form of charismatic provision for needs. From the point of view of
rational economic activity, charisma is a typical anti-economic force.
It repudiates any sort of involvement in the everyday routine world.
It can only tolerate, with an attitude of complete emotional indifference, irregular, unsystematic, acquisitive acts. In that it relieves the
recipient of economic concerns, dependence on property income can
be the economic basis of a charismatic mode of life for some groups;
but that is not usually acceptable for the normal charismatic 'revolutionary.'

The fact that incumbency of church office has been forbidden to
the Jesuits is a rationalized application of this principle of discipleship. The fact that all the 'virtuosi' of asceticism, the mendicant
orders, and fighters for a faith belong in this category, is quite clear.
Almost all prophets have been supported by voluntary gifts. The well-
known saying of St. Paul, 'If a man does not work, neither shall he
eat,' was directed against the swarm of charismatic missionaries. It
obviously has nothing to do with a positive valuation of economic
activity for its own sake, but only lays it down as a duty of each individual somehow to provide for his own support. This because he
realized that the purely charismatic parable of the lilies of the field
was not capable of literal application, but at best 'taking no thought
for the morrow' could be hoped for. On the other hand, in such a
case as primarily an artistic type of charismatic discipleship, it is conceivable that insulation from economic struggle should mean limita-
tion of those who were really eligible to the 'economically independent'; that is, to persons living on income from property. This has been
true of the circle of Stefan George, at least in its primary intentions.

5. In traditionally stereotyped periods, charisma is the greatest
revolutionary force. The equally revolutionary force of 'reason' works
from without by altering the situations of action, and hence its problems finally in this way changing men's attitudes toward them; or it
intellectualizes the individual. Charisma, on the other hand, may
involve a subjective or internal reorientation born out of suffering,
conflicts, or enthusiasm. It may then result in a radical alteration of
the central system of attitudes and directions of action with a completely new orientation of all attitudes toward the different problems

and structures of the 'world.'[8] In prerationalistic periods, tradition and charisma between them have almost exhausted the whole of the orientation of action.

[8] Weber here uses *Welt* in quotation marks, indicating that it refers to its meaning in what is primarily a religious context. It is the sphere of 'worldly' things and interests as distinguished from transcendental religious interests.—ED. [Parsons' footnote]

7

The Political Scene*

Our foreign interests are essentially conditioned. We are a power-State. For every power-State the proximity of another power-State means a restriction on the liberty of its own political decision, because it must show consideration for the other power-State. For each power-State it is desirable to be surrounded by possibly weak States or at least by as few other power-States as possible. Fate has ordained (*gefügt*) that only Germany borders three great land powers, and the three greatest after us, and moreover one of these is the greatest sea-power. Thus Germany is in their way. No other country on earth has to face such a situation. [p. 16]

With nations like the English to whom the dependence of their economic success on their political power situation is not daily demonstrated, the instincts for these specific political interests are not present, at least not generally, within the great masses of the nation which have to struggle for the necessities of daily life—it would be unjust to ask for these instincts here. Yet in great moments, in case of war, the significance of national power strikes their soul—then, they realize that the national state rests on genuine (*urwuechsigen*) psychological foundations, also with the economically dominated large groups of the nation. Furthermore that the nation is not only the superstructure (*Ueberbau*), simply the organization of the economically dominating groups. In normal times this political instinct of the masses becomes unconscious. Then it is the specific function

* From J. P. Mayer, *Max Weber and German Politics: A Study in Political Sociology* (London: Faber and Faber Ltd., 1944). The selections are arranged in chronological order to a large extent, and most of them are from Weber's collection of political essays (*Gesammelte Politische Schriften*). The translations from Weber are by Mayer.

of the economically and politically leading groups to be bearers of the political sense (*Sinnes*), the sole reason to justify them politically. [p. 33]

It is dangerous and in the long run incompatible with the interest of the nation if an economically declining class holds political power, but it is even more dangerous if classes, towards which economic power and henceforth aspiration to political power is moving, are politically not yet mature for political leadership. [p. 34]

The estates of the east were the protective points of the dominating class disseminated all over Prussia; they formed the point d'appui of the civil service, yet irresistibly with the social decline of the Junkers, the gravitation point of the political intelligentsia moves to the towns. [p. 34]

The reason for the political immaturity of broad masses of the German bourgeoisie is to be found in its political past. The political education of a century cannot be made good within one decade, and the domination of a great man [Bismarck] is not always a means of political education. The serious question now for the political future of the German bourgeoisie is: Is it too late to make good this lack of political education? No economic factor can replace it. [p. 35]

. . . a revolution from below is not possible without the assistance or the tolerance of the bourgeoisie, likewise a canalization from above is not possible without its support. [p. 45]

Everywhere the framework of a new bondage is ready, waiting only for the slowing down of technical "progress" and for the victory of as yet "free" territory and "free" markets, to make the masses tractable to its compulsion. At the same time the increasing complexity of the economic system, its partial nationalization or "municipalization", and the territorial magnitude of national organisms, is creating ever more clerical work, an increasing specialization of labor and professional training in administration—and this means the creation of a bureaucratic cast. . . . Whatever spheres of "inalienable" personality and freedom are still unwon by the common people in the course of the next few generations, and while the economic and intellectual "revolution", the much-maligned "subjectivism" (by which, and by which alone, the individual has been made self-dependent), still remains unbroken, may perhaps—once the world has become economically "full" and intellectually "sated" remain unachieved by them, for as far as our weak eyes can pierce the impenetrable mists of the future of mankind. . . . [p. 46]

At no price . . . the dangerously ready formula: For the Kaiser against the Centre Party with its lust for power. Such a policy would revenge itself terribly. The degree of contempt with which we are met as a nation abroad (in Italy, U.S.A., everywhere) and justified contempt—that is decisive—because we tolerate the regime of this man, has become a power-factor of first-class significance in world policy. . . . No man and no party which cultivates democratic and national ideals should accept responsibility for this regime whose continuation threatens our position in the world more than any colonial problem whatsoever. We should blame and oppose the Centre party *not* because it questions "the power of command" of the Kaiser or even less because it aimed for power according to the number of its deputies, for control of the colonial administration, for parliamentary co-government (*Nebenregierung*). The Centre Party is to blame because it has, as the dominating party in Parliament, advanced and supported the system of *sham* constitutionalism. . . . It has maintained a "parliamentary patronage" behind the scenes: the sugar candy by which since a decade the dominating parties, Centre Party, but likewise Conservatives and National Liberals, have been incorporated into the dominating personal regime of our sham constitutionalism. . . . [p. 47]

The dynasty of the Hohenzollern knows only the corporal's form of power: to command, to obey, to stand at attention, to boast. [p. 49]

Every bureaucracy has the tendency to increase, thereby achieving the same effect. Thus our contemporary German bureaucracy. And while in the Ancient World the policy of the polis had to be the 'pacemaker' for capitalism, to-day capitalism is the pace-maker for bureaucratizing the economic system. Let us imagine that coal, iron, all mining and metallurgic products, in addition alcoholic products, sugar, tobacco, matches, in short all mass products, to-day already produced by cartels, taken over by State or State-controlled enterprises, more over, the State-run controlled big estates multiplied. . .

workshops and co-operatives for the needs of army and State officials
also administered by the State, inland and foreign shipping controlled
by the State, also all railways, etc. . . . and all these enterprises held
in bureaucratic order, . . . all the rest corporatively with numerous
qualifications academic and otherwise, the type of the *rentier paisible*
generalized—thus under a militarist-dynastic regime, the position prevailing under the later Roman Emperors would be achieved best on
technically more advanced foundations. The modern German bourgeois has not more in common with the qualities of his ancestors
during the period of the late Middle Ages than had the Athenian
under the Roman Emperors with his ancestors who fought at Mara-
thon. "Order" is his slogan, in most cases also when he is a "Social
Democrat". With regard to our society it is highly probable that
bureaucratization will master capitalism—*some time*, as it happened
in antiquity. So "order" will replace "anarchy of production", similar
in principle as under the Roman Emperors, or even more so under
the Ptolemies or during the "new Egyptian Empire", and let no one
believe that to serve in an army, bureaucratized and provided with
war machines, drilled in barracks, could offer a counter-weight, or
that the modern military robot within dynastic States should have
any connection with the civic military spirit of the past. [p. 54]

I do not care about the form of the State, if only politicians and
not dilettante fools like Wilhelm II and the like rule the country.
. . . I see now no other way than ruthless parliamentarization—
quand-même, to freeze out these people. The civil servants must be
subordinated to parliament. Altogether and without exception. They
are technicians. . . . Forms of State are for me techniques like any
other machinery. I would attack parliament and defend the monarch,
if the latter were a politician. . . . [p. 58]

In a modern state, real power, which acts not through parliamentary speeches nor through the pronouncements of the Crown, but
through everyday administration, lies necessarily and inevitably in the
hands of the bureaucracy, both military and civil. For the modern
officer of high rank even directs battles from his desk. [p. 60]

This fundamental principle . . . the separation of the worker
from the means of production in the economic sphere, from the

means of waging war in the army, the means of administration in
public service, money in all spheres, the means of research in universities and laboratories is the common and basic foundation of a
modern power-political and military state and of capitalist private
enterprise. In both cases direction of power lies in the hands of that
authority, which the bureaucracy (judges, civil servants, officers, fore-
men, clerks, non-commissioned officers) either directly or indirectly
obeys. It is a characteristic feature of all these institutions, whose
existence and function, both in theory and practice, is inseparably
bound up with this concentration of the means of production. [p. 61]

[The] position [of Lloyd George, the British Prime Minister in
World War I,] rests as a matter of fact not on the confidence of parliament and its parties, but on the confidence of the masses of the
country and of the fighting army. Parliament accepts . . . this situation. There is, therefore, a contrast between plebiscitary and parliamentary selection of political leaders. But that does not mean that
Parliament is useless. In England it acts as a guarantee against the
plebiscitarian trustee of the masses (1) by continuity, and (2) by
the controlling power of its position; (3) by the guarantee and main-
tenance of citizens' rights against him; (4) by a regular political safe-
guard against politicians using parliamentary business to win the
favor of the masses for themselves; (5) by peaceful means of eliminating "dictators" who lose the support of the masses.

This breakdown of Ludendorff, the demoralization of the army; a
consequence of this permanent whipping up of Stimmung by prom-
ises which it was impossible to fulfil, this short-sightedness and complete lack of dignity of the Kaiser and giddiness of our dilettante
government—all this was painful. It will take a long time for us to
swallow this blow to our honour, and the intoxication of the "Revolution" [of 1918] is now only a kind of narcotic for the people, before
the great misery begins. Awful are those empty words and depressing
those vague hopes, and this totally dilettante play, with a "happier
future" which never was further from realization. I am only glad
about the humble matter-of-factness (schlichte Sachlichkeit) of the
simple trade union people, and also of many soldiers—of our workers' and soldiers' "soviet" to which I belong. They have done their
work excellently; this I must say without question. The nation as a

whole is disciplined, but, once this discipline is threatened, then everything, that is clear, is threatened, even the soul of these people. [p. 71]

We have indeed no cause to love the masters of heavy industry. It is one of the main tasks of democracy to break the dangerous political influence which they had on the old political regime. Yet economically their achievements cannot be dispensed with, even less so when as just now the whole economic system has to be reorganized. The *Communist Manifesto* has rightly stressed the economically— not politically—revolutionary character of the work of the bourgeois capitalistic entrepreneurs. No trade union, still less no state socialist official, can replace the functions of the capitalists. One must apply them only at the right place; offer them the unavoidable premium of profit, but not allow them to become stronger than democracy. . . . [p. 73]

The early Christians knew very well that the world is full of devils, and that he who enters politics, e.g. the realm where alone power and violence as means are valid, concludes a pact with devilish powers, and that from good may only come good, from evil only evil is *not* true; but very often the contrary. Who does not see this is politically a child. [p. 89]

The genius or demon of politics . . . lives with the God of love, and also with the God of the Church in an inner tension which at any time may break out into an unsolvable conflict. . . . [p. 89]

Politics is like digging slowly and steadily into hard ground, with both enthusiasm and judgment. History proves that you will not be able to achieve what is possible if you do not strive sometimes after the impossible. The man who undertakes this must be a leader and not only a leader but also—using the word in its literal sense—a hero. Those who do not possess either of these qualities must arm themselves with that stoutness of heart which gives hope even to desperate men, or they will not even be able to achieve what is already possible. Only he who is certain that he will not despair when the world, as he sees it, is too stupid and too mean to appreciate what he is offering it, and who is prepared to persevere, only he should take up politics as a profession. [p. 90]